ANALYZING TH

CRITICAL PERSPECTIVES ON IMMIGRANTS AND REFUGEES

Edited by Anne C. Cunningham

Enslow Publishing
101 W. 23rd Street
Suite 240
New York, NY 10011
USA

enslow.com

Published in 2017 by Enslow Publishing, LLC
101 W. 23rd Street, Suite 240, New York, NY 10011

Library of Congress Cataloging-in-Publication Data

Names: Cunningham, Anne C.
Title: Critical perspectives on immigrants and refugees / edited by Anne C. Cunningham.
Description: New York : Enslow Publishing, 2017 | Series: Analyzing the issues | Includes bibliographical references and index.
Identifiers: ISBN 9780766076778 (library bound)
Subjects: LCSH: Immigrants—United States—Juvenile literature. | United States—Emigration and immigration—Juvenile literature. | Refugees—United States—Juvenile literature.
Classification: LCC JV6455.C746 2017 | DDC 325.73—dc23

Printed in the United States of America

To Our Readers: We have done our best to make sure all website addresses in this book were active and appropriate when we went to press. However, the author and the publisher have no control over and assume no liability for the material available on those websites or on any websites they may link to. Any comments or suggestions can be sent by e-mail to customerservice@enslow.com.

Excerpts and articles have been reproduced with the permission of the copyright holders.

CONTENTS

INTRODUCTION

The movement of individuals, families, tribes, and larger social units across both political borders and geographic boundaries is a story nearly as old as humanity itself. This phenomenon, known generally as migration, occurs when a group sets off to permanently resettle in a new location and thus excludes temporary relocation or nomadic patterns. Migration can be triggered by several root causes: loss of food supply, hostile invasion, climate, and religious or social conflict, among other catalysts.

Broadly speaking, migration can be either voluntary or involuntary. Economic migrants, those in search of better labor prospects and a higher standard of living, are by far the most common type of migrants. All economically motivated migration is considered voluntary, regardless of how dire the circumstances from which the migrants flee. Involuntary migration, on the other hand, is the forcible capture and transport of people against their will. This abusive practice is less common today, but it continues in some parts of the globe in the form of ethnic cleansing.

Historically, involuntary migration has been a foundational part of the American social structure. Perhaps even eclipsing the genial image of the European immigrant arriving at Ellis Island, shameful examples of African slaves brought to toil on North American plantations and Native Americans pushed to reservations remain blights on a mythical America "built by immigrants." We must fully acknowledge the nation's checkered origins to gain a more complete picture of how, by whom, and at whose expense America was truly developed.

Refugees are a specific, rigorously defined, and quickly growing subset of involuntary migrants. As defined by the US Immigration and Nationality Act, a refugee "is a person who is unable or unwilling to return to his or her home country because of a 'well-founded fear of persecution' due to race, membership in a particular social group, political opinion, religion, or national origin."[1] It is notable that US law excludes the large numbers of environmental migrants displaced by climate change and other natural disasters from the category of refugee, although environmental migrants are eligible for resettlement through the office of the United Nations High Commissioner on Refugees. Complicating matters is that often, as in the case of the current Syrian refugee crisis, the causes are multiple: climate change causes a drought, which destabilizes rural populations and worsens political unrest. In this situation, any meaningful distinction between socially constructed versus "natural" conditions breaks down—the unfortunate result is a cycle of misery that does not lend itself to easy solutions.

Indeed, as some writers we will shortly examine attest, the difference between voluntary and involuntary immigration is only subjective. In the opening article of this reader, Judith Reed argues for a greatly expanded classification of involuntary immigrants. In her view, those from poorer nations displaced by economic conditions favorable to corporate free trade (as opposed to fair trade) have as much of a right to claim refugee status as those fleeing political persecution. Regardless of semantic labels regarding a migrant's relative agency, Reed suggests compassion for those victimized by employers who are free to move wherever labor conditions are cheapest and most favorable and without accountability to the nations and workers left behind.

In the United States today, we tend to view issues surrounding immigration and refugees as a set of trade-offs. In Chapter 4, Philip Cafaro articulates what's at stake in these choices. He argues that unsustainable population growth is already wreaking environmental havoc and that more immigration will make matters worse. But immigrants also contribute much to the economic and cultural health of the country. In fact, multiple studies show that first-generation immigrants are less likely to engage in criminal behavior than native-born Americans.

Immigration is beneficial, but many argue we can't return to the open borders that existed prior to 1965. Thus, the question becomes how to set fair limits on immigration. President Obama elevates the law as his primary criterion. Those who abide by it should be allowed to remain in the country, but those who break it will be deported. As we will see, fair outcomes from this approach will depend on how our beliefs regarding criminality are applied in practice. Concerning refugees, the trade-off tends to be framed as a tension between national security and humanitarian values. Tracing our attitudes toward refugees historically, a pattern of favoring security over humanitarianism emerges as a relative constant.

American public opinion and the US political system reflect these ambivalences. Although there is widespread support for modest immigration reform such as the DREAM Act, the political force necessary to pass such a law has never materialized. And on the score of refugees, each new international incident makes Americans less willing to help those in need, who ironically are often victims of the same forces we oppose. The articles that follow address and untangle these ambiguities. In a topic rife with emotional and xenophobic responses, critical analysis and sensitivity to rhetoric is essential to formulate nuanced and ethical positions.

CHAPTER 1

WHAT THE EXPERTS AND ACADEMICS SAY

The debate about immigrants and refugees generally focuses on policies, quotas, national security, and other details concerning the "host" nation's laws and attitudes toward newcomers seeking asylum—who usually leave their countries under extreme duress. As a result, much-needed context often goes missing from analysis. Given that every day, staggering amounts of people risk their life savings, safety, and possibly even their lives traveling to foreign nations in search of better prospects, it behooves us to understand the complex historical forces shaping migration on a global level. Moreover, these forces also structure the ways in which immigration and refugees affect our economy and culture domestically.

Judith Reed's article, "Immigrants as Refugees of the Global Economy: Learning to Teach (About) Today's Migrants," argues that corporate interests and capitalism have enriched the global north but underdeveloped and exploited the global south. Although political unrest, religious conflict, and climate change are primary drivers of migration, Reed concludes that we must come to terms with colonialism's legacy of unequal wealth distribution and asymmetric power relations to fully understand the ongoing refugee and migration crisis. While her essay is aimed at future teachers, the implications are sufficiently broad to merit prominent inclusion in this reader.

On the domestic front, a study republished here shows that first-generation immigrants are less likely to engage in criminal behavior than native-born Americans or second-generation immigrants. This study, and many studies like it, flies in the face of media discourse linking immigrants with higher crime rates. Finally, the last two articles in this chapter will turn to the global refugee crisis and examine the difference between migrants and refugees, as well as European responses to this crisis.

"IMMIGRANTS AS REFUGEES OF THE GLOBAL ECONOMY: LEARNING TO TEACH (ABOUT) TODAY'S MIGRANTS," BY JUDITH REED, FROM *MULTICULTURAL EDUCATION*, MARCH 22, 2015

IMMIGRATION AND THE GLOBAL ECONOMY

The phenomenon of migration as we know it today must be understood in the larger context of the globalized economy and the "race to the bottom" that characterizes the multinational corporate relationship with the global South. A deeper understanding of the ways in which migration today is rooted in the machinations of the globalized economy can help engender compassion and solidarity.

Media portrayal of recent immigrants in general and undocumented immigrants in particular infects not just educational policy but the attitudes of the public toward massive numbers of rudely dislocated human beings—"Immigrants are taking our jobs!" "They are wanton lawbreakers!" As teachers, we are in a position to combat such perceptions through our curricula and to foster an inclusive community that recognizes the desperate needs of refugees from the globalized economy.

Without understanding the forces compelling immigration into the U.S. today, teachers are at risk of falling prey to the dominant narrative advanced by media and corporate interests, to the detriment of children from immigrant families. Teachers need compassion for the struggles faced by these students and their parents in their communities and elsewhere. Further, teachers who are committed to advancing equity and social justice through their teaching must stand prepared with both courage and knowledge to counter the dominant narrative in their teaching.

This article investigates a curriculum unit for pre-service teachers that rests upon a study of the globalized economy and the international "race to the bottom." Students are asked to consider whether the effects on human lives brought about by free trade agreements and third world debt in fact amounts to a kind of violence. Is the loss of a livelihood through these means really much different from losses brought about by other destructive conditions such as war or drought? When people are forced to migrate in order to escape intolerable and life-threatening conditions, should it matter whether this was caused by acts of nature or by institutions and policies created to protect the interests of transnational capital? And ultimately, how should we teach children and youth about immigration today?

A "DIVERSITY" COURSE FOR PRE-SERVICE TEACHERS

I teach the "diversity" course for undergraduate elementary and early childhood majors at a public liberal arts college in New England. Typically taken in the sophomore year, the course is required prior to methods coursework with its accompanying practicum. In its former iteration, this course was the typical survey of the various ways in which humans can be "different." It was, and still is, an attempt to foster culturally responsive educators, but two of my colleagues and I redesigned it to emphasize the role played by historical-political-economic forces over the last 500 years.

The aim is to equip students better to interrogate the dominant narrative and ultimately to prepare them to expose its shortcomings and omissions to their future students. The course in its entirety includes the following:

- Economic inequity in the U.S. today, and why capitalism produces wealth inequality.
- The role of public education in re-producing class-based inequity (including NCLB and the move to privatize public education).
- The still-ongoing history of Native American conquest and subjugation.
- The ongoing history of African American inequality in the U.S.
- Current forces affecting and surrounding immigration into the U.S.
- Organizing for change.

Our students are predominantly female and White. They have to take this course quite early in their studies, with little if any prior practical experience. They are eager to learn how to be good teachers (in their view of "good teaching"). Perhaps understandably, many are a bit impatient (some more than a bit) with a course requirement that on the surface doesn't appear to be teaching them how to do that.

COLONIAL ROOTS

The topic of modern migration and immigration, which is addressed in three weeks of class near the end of the semester, is the subject of this article. Early on in the course, we have revisited the Columbus myth, and now we return to the theme of colonialism. By way of introduction, I ask my students to speculate on why some countries in the world have huge concentrations of wealth, while others are deeply impoverished. Their conjectures predictably reflect the dominant thinking: corrupt governments, natural disasters and war, lack of natural resources, and so on.

I then ask them to list as many countries as possible that are relatively poor, and to make a second list of the wealthy nations in the world. We compile the two lists on the board, and I ask them to identify the continents where most of the wealthy countries are located, and then where most of the poor countries are found. Also, what relationships have existed historically between those on the wealthy list and those that are impoverished? Sometimes students are totally stumped, but usually someone eventually mentions colonization. In any case, I then send them off to read the chapter on colonialism in Bill Bigelow's and Bob Peterson's (2002) *Rethinking Globalization*.

Thus begins the realization that today's wealthy countries gained their wealth (in short) by taking it from today's poor countries—most of whom, by the way, were anything but destitute before the plunder began. This sets the stage for an explanation of how such a large proportion of the world's population have come to live in conditions of extreme poverty, when 500 years ago their ancestors enjoyed conditions of sufficiency, even plenty, and often in civilizations that were arguably more advanced than European society at the time.

Here we have a crack at debunking American exceptionalism and Eurocentrism, and also take a poke at

White supremacy. (In this regard, it is important to under-score the role played in the Americas by the spread of disease, which literally decimated the population of the hemisphere well in advance of the conquest by suppos-edly "superior" armaments.)

THE GLOBALIZED ECONOMY

"Colonialism without colonies" (Bigelow and Peterson, 2002) well describes the methodology for continuing the exploitation of the Global South by the North in modern times. I introduce this topic with a short but powerful film called *The Hidden Face of Globalization* (Darpon, 2003), featuring women in Bangladeshi sweatshops who are paid 17 cents an hour, working 20-hour days to manufacture clothing for companies like Disney and Walmart. Students investigate the labels on the clothing they happen to be wearing to see where in the world other people may have labored to produce it, much like the women in the video.

Next we engage in a simulation role play to illus-trate the corporate "race to the bottom" that results in the conditions under which those young women in Bangla-desh labor to fashion our clothing and most of the other items we depend on and can readily acquire. Developed by Bill Bigelow (2002, 2006), the "Transnational Capital Auction" allows students to play the role of leaders in anonymous third world countries. They compete to attract transnational corporate investment by adjusting labor, taxation, and environmental laws and policies so as to be maximally "friendly to capital."

Through class discussions and mini-lectures along with further readings from *Rethinking Globalization*

(Bigelow & Peterson, 2002), students learn about the role of the World Bank, the International Monetary Fund (IMF), and the World Trade Organization (WTO) in constructing the globalized economy and supporting the interests of transnational corporations. They learn about free trade agreements and the meaning of "free trade" as opposed to "fair trade." They are introduced to neoliberal and "trickle-down" economic theory. They read about child labor, sweatshops, and migrant labor. They learn about the devastation of local agriculture in the Global South wreaked by industrial agriculture hand in hand with the World Bank, the IMF, and the WTO.

FORCED MIGRATION

While in itself this material is arguably important to any educated citizen living in today's world, it is crucial foundational knowledge for understanding the forces impelling most of today's migration from Global South to North. In order to build solidarity with the immigrant population that is crossing our southern border, students like mine will need to see clearly how these migrants are virtually forced to leave behind all that they know and love, facing untold dangers to enter an unknown land where prospects are uncertain at best.

We begin this last phase of the unit with another chance to speculate. "Imagine yourself," I say, "in the place of someone who has decided to leave the home where you were born and where you have friends and family, and go away to find work in another country where you have never been before, where you don't speak the language, and where you don't know anyone. The journey to get there is very expensive and very dangerous, and you might not get there alive. What do you imagine might be the reasons for doing such a thing?"

On the board we list all the reasons students can come up with: war, famine, wanting a better opportunity, needing a job, and so on. We then watch a half-hour video called *Uprooted: Refugees of the Global Economy* (Nilsen, 2001), which features the stories of a young woman from the Philippines, a couple from Bolivia, and a man from Haiti. Some students are asked to focus on noting the systemic reasons for large numbers of people like these to leave their homes and families and friends for other countries. Others are asked to focus on the personal reasons why the individual people featured in the film left home and family and friends to come to the U.S.

Afterwards, we list these two types of reasons. The video includes systemic factors such as the crushing national debt imposed by the IMF and World Bank, a lack of hard currency to pay back the debt, crippling inflation, the loss of domestic industry due to underselling by cheap imports from the North, and loss of jobs as corporations pull out of one impoverished country to relocate in another. Personal factors help put a human face on the systemic. One family loses their life savings in a scam that falsely promises to take the father safely to the U.S., leaving the eldest daughter to forego college in favor of life as a domestic drudge in thrall to a wealthy U.S. family, sending half her meager earnings home each month to help her own family.

We discuss these reasons and the three stories. How do they compare to the reasons students imagined?

How much choice did the people in the video have in leaving home? In entering the U.S. without the required documents? Why did they not have those documents?

In another of Bill Bigelow's (2006) well-crafted activities, students create short improvisational skits to explore some of the real-life dilemmas that such migrants have faced, and still do. They also search alternative news sources such as *truthout.org* and *Democracy Now!* to bring in articles on migrant labor in the U.S. and on the education of unauthorized immigrant children.

In a final bid to build solidarity with (or at least to engender compassion for) the refugees of the global economy, I show a video by Jenny Alexander (2007) documenting a recent immigration raid on a factory in New Bedford, Massachusetts, not that far from our campus. Women who were working in a factory manufacturing backpacks for the U.S. military were swept up summarily, shackled and handcuffed, and treated like criminals. Many were subjected to deportation, including mothers separated from their nursing babies and small children.

Ultimately, students are invited to consider the meaning of the term "refugee." To what extent might it appropriately be applied to people whose livelihoods are endangered by economic forces, the effects of which they cannot mitigate, and which they can only minimally avoid by migrating elsewhere? Is it appropriate that people fleeing war or political imprisonment may be granted refugee status, while others, also imperiled in their homelands but by different factors, are denied that status?

TEACHING ABOUT IMMIGRATION

At the end of each unit of study in the course, students have an opportunity to consider how they might teach about that topic to their future students. This is an important feature in the course, as it helps students to find the connections between the course material and their future work with young children. It helps allay their impatience with an education course that tasks them to learn about economics, history and other topics that may seem superfluous to their career goals. It also helps them see that controversial topics, even tragic ones, are not only possible to bring into early childhood and elementary classrooms, but necessary, if we are to avoid repeating the disinformation that passed for schooling in our own upbringing.

For this unit, I bring to class a variety of children's literature on the topic of modern day immigration and migrant labor. (A bibliography is provided in the Appendix that follows this article. [*Editor's note: the appendix is included in the chapter notes.*]) In teams, students select a book around which to base a lesson or mini-unit, rough out their plans, and then present the results to the rest of the class.

All of these children's books can open up discussion of hardships endured by migrant children and their families. Some touch on language learning, and additionally on the relative difficulty that adults may experience in acquiring a new language compared with their children, who then may be forced into an intermediary role between parent and other adults (Elya, 2002). Some are written in both Spanish and English (Anzaldua, 1993;

Dorros, 1993; Perez, 2002). A few unabashedly take on the issue of unauthorized entry into the United States (Anzaldua, 1993). The many migrant workers who are native born U.S. citizens are represented (Krull, 2003; Smothers, 2003). The winning of rights for migrant farm workers in the U.S. is included (Krull, 2003). Many reflect the deep and abiding love that these displaced families hold for the homeland they are forced to flee (Bunting, 1996; Perez, 2002; Thomas, 1994). All of these topics, and others, can be discussed in the context of the students' presentations in class.

IMPACT ON STUDENTS

Students write responses to a set of essay questions at the end of each unit of study in the course. For this final unit, the culminating essay question is posed as follows:

> Free trade policies have created conditions where capital (i.e., corporate investment) is free to cross national boundaries at will, seeking the most profitable regions in which to operate (e.g., where wages are lowest, worker safety laws and environmental laws are non-existent or not enforced, child labor is allowed, etc.).

> *As long as that is the case*, do you believe that labor (i.e., human beings) should be equally free to cross national boundaries in order to escape conditions of poverty and exploitation created by these free trade policies?

I tell the students that this question is an opinion piece, and there are no right or wrong answers, as long as their opinions are well-reasoned and supported.

A majority of students are in favor of allowing labor the same freedom of movement that capital enjoys: One student wrote:

> I believe that as long as developed countries and companies are allowed to go over to the third world countries and take advantage of the desperate need of income to survive and to abuse and treat the workers inhumanely, the people from these countries should have the equal right to cross the boundaries to escape these conditions that are forcing them into extreme poverty. It's only right that if companies and free trade are creating even more impoverished countries, then the people have a choice to escape the exploitation and poverty.
>
> Poor people are prevented from coming to the U.S. because the rights of corporations are favored over people's needs to survive and escape their poverty-ridden countries. If they were allowed to cross national boundaries freely, just as capital can, there wouldn't be such trouble climbing out of poverty and it may even help poverty throughout the world because there would be no people to force into it.

A second student agreed, but hopes fair trade might somehow (magically?) replace free trade, obviating the need for migration

> We have been responsible for the failing economy of several countries due to globalization. Free trade policies have created conditions of poverty and exploitation in third world countries. There is no work or economic opportunity for the people of

these countries because the global economy has depleted all the resources these counties once had. The people that the United States and other developed nations have taken advantage of for centuries should be able to try and dig themselves, their families and their countries out of debt by working under fair conditions in these first world nations. If the global economy can come in [to a third world country] and make structural changes to the entire economic system, then the people of [those] countries should be equally free to reap the benefits of another country's economy and resources. However, contrary to this belief I think that the real solution is in fair trade and similar practices. It would be most beneficial if these third world countries were able to restore their economies and trading markets so that they are equally benefited by the globalized economy and trade. This is almost unimaginable, but steering away from free trade policies and toward fair trade would keep migrant workers from needing to leave their own homes for work and allow them to support their own nations' economy rather than the one that crippled them to begin with.

Some students believe that immigration wreaks havoc in the U.S. This student sees this as an irritant that might motivate change for the better:

If the people from these third world countries started crossing borders as they please and coming to the northern more civic [sic] countries, taking jobs from their people and causing upheaval, then maybe something would begin to change in the way the WTO operates.

Some students would like to have it both ways:

I believe that if these people are just going out of their country to escape these living conditions, then they should be equally free to do so. I do not feel that they should be able to freely come to the United States, though, unless authorized... because we already have enough people here. With the amount of people here, there already is not enough work for them, let alone these individuals. Not only that, but we have not even made schooling good enough in some areas for our kids. So, to add more unauthorized people would not be fair to the people here.

Others are firm in their opinion that, even given current conditions, free migration from impoverished countries to wealthy ones is not acceptable:

I do not see how a person could not be against free trade and want to continue to enable corporations to continue to treat workers in such an inhuman fashion.... However, I do not believe that the solution would be allowing people to be free to cross national boundaries in order to escape conditions of poverty...Unfortunately, most of the time immigrants have a difficult time escaping poverty even after coming to the U.S...If everyone were free to cross the borders there would be a large amount of individuals flooding in the U.S. All of these individuals would have a difficult time finding work... [Also,] opening up the borders would cause the home countries' economies...[to] crash.

As much as it is nice to think we can let people cross the border to work and escape problems in their country, that is just not realistic. This country has protected borders for a reason and although it seems ideal to help everyone, we can't have everyone escaping to the United States. Obviously what happens in other countries isn't ok and is really unfortunate, but we can't take everyone into this country. [We] can't afford to have them and they really can't afford to be here. Sooner or later the amount of work would run out, Americans would lose their jobs to the people who immigrated and would work for cheaper. These protected workers keep the United States as successful as it is…The United States needs to continue having protected borders because before we can think of others we have to think of our own problems first, which we seem to have many of.

Some students reject the premise of the question. (Fair enough!) However, this student then goes on to blame the victim:

I do not believe that either party should be able to cross borders…The world should focus more on improving the life and economy of every country, not just instilling efforts into first world countries in the hope that those few countries on top of the world economy will be able to and responsible for taking care of every human on earth in need of a stable economy and safe living and working environment. This expectation is unreasonable. Countries such as India, Bolivia, the Philippines and Haiti need to stop letting United States forces come in and take over. Allowing richer countries to enslave native peoples somewhere else will certainly not bring wealth to those countries they enslave. I do not know what those third world country leaders are thinking. Perhaps they are desperate for resources and money [so] that they think that letting the U.S. take over for a while will be a quick fix. This is false. The U.S. has a way of taking over and staying where they want to keep power…The World Bank and World Trade Organization need to be stood up to. They bully countries into thinking that they need to be part of the club to be successful. 'Let America take over and build factories in your country and enslave your already impoverished people and then you will be magically lifted out of poverty.' Why do countries believe this? The third world countries need to be educated in what is going on in the world and team up to fight against greater first world forces. Find the flaw in their system and end the 'free' trade that restricts most of the world.

Nonetheless, within this last student's diatribe lies the germ of an interesting idea. "The third world countries," she suggests, "need to…*team up* to fight against greater first world forces" (emphasis added).

ANALYSIS AND SUMMARY

What do these comments reveal about the results of this three-week investigation into the workings of the globalized economy, and in particular its effects on workers and migration? Clearly, most students still have not fully grasped the fact that transnational capital has become a hegemonic force. Many don't see that solutions like "steering away" from free trade and toward fair trade is a fantasy, as long as the current economic system persists, with transnational capital at the helm, doing all the steering. Others berate the third world countries for not standing up to bullies like the U.S., and (echoing the myth of the welfare queen) simultaneously for expecting the wealthy countries to "take care of every human on earth." Some continue to fear that looser immigration restrictions may "flood the U.S." and "Americans [sic] would lose their jobs."

On the other hand, most of these students have learned a great deal. They are clear about the devastating effects on the third world of European colonialism, to the vast benefit of Europeans and their descendants in the western hemisphere. They are conversant with the terms of the globalized economy and understand that it has continued the ruinous work of colonization, but now without the need for actual colonies. They are disabused of the illusion that impoverished migrants are thrilled to leave their own homelands, or that the United States is a land of golden opportunity for all.

They understand that the immigration story of today is not the old Ellis Island story, and there is hope that if and when they teach about immigration it will not be that story that they tell. There is ample evidence of their increased compassion for (and maybe even solidarity with) the refugees of the global economy who fill the meanest positions in our workforce and whose children they will no doubt encounter in their future classrooms.

1. Does the author's assessment of a global "race to the bottom" appear accurate to you? Do you agree that corporate power and capital-friendly transnational organizations such as the World Bank and the International Monetary Fund have made life in the global south untenable, thus, forcing migration? Why or why not?

2. Do you think it is fair to liken actual refugees from war-torn failed states to "economic" refugees?

"CRIME RISES AMONG SECOND-GENERATION IMMIGRANTS AS THEY ASSIMILATE," BY RICH MORIN, FROM THE PEW RESEARCH CENTER, OCTOBER 15, 2012

Why does the crime rate soar among second-generation immigrants compared with their foreign-born peers? Until recently, most sociologists have explained this increase by noting that many second-generation immigrants feel caught between two conflicting worlds—the old world of their parents and the new world of their birth.

But recently researchers have posited an alternate theory: Second-generation immigrants are just "catching up" with the rest of us, claims Bianca E. Bersani, a sociologist at the University of Massachusetts-Boston.

Call it the dark side of assimilation. These second-generation immigrants have become as susceptible to temptation and harmful influences as are other Americans according to Bersani. The unhappy consequence is a similar likelihood of committing a crime, Bersani wrote in an article published online by the journal Crime & Delinquency.

Other studies have documented how second-generation immigrants have become more like the typical American, both in positive and negative ways. For example, a Pew Research Center analysis of Census data earlier this year found that median family income of second-generation immigrants is virtually identical to the national median and higher than their foreign-born counterparts. Home ownership rates follow a similar trajectory.

In her study, Bersani analyzed crime data collected from first- and second-generation immigrants. She then compared those crime rates with the other native-born adults and found striking similarities between second-generation immigrants and native-born non-Hispanic whites.

She begins her analysis by noting this well-documented phenomenon: The crime rate among first-generation immigrants—those who came to this country from somewhere else—is significantly lower than the overall crime rate and that of the second generation. It's even lower for those in their teens and early 20s, the age range when criminal involvement peaks.

But just a generation later, the crime rate soars. In fact, it is virtually identical to the rate among native-born Americans across the most crime-prone years. As an earlier Bersani study shows, about a quarter of 16-year-old native-born and second-generation immigrants have committed a crime in the past year. In contrast, about 17% of the foreign-born 16-year olds have broken the law.

WHAT EXPLAINS THE DIFFERENCE?

Some researchers say the generations face two different sets of experiences, with the second generation—those with at least one parent who was born abroad—caught in the middle. They argue the second generation is caught between conflicting family and social values and expectations, and one result of this old world/new world conflict is a greater propensity to commit crime.

To explore the causes of crime among second-generation immigrants, Besani used data from the Bureau of Labor Statistics National Longitudinal Survey of Youth 1997, a household-based, representative sample of people living in the U.S. in 1997 who were born from 1980 through 1984. The initial sample includes 8,984 youth who have been interviewed on an annual basis beginning in 1997. The dataset she used contained data collected through 2005.

The survey questioned respondents on sensitive topics, including the number of times they had a purposely damaged or destroyed property, committed a theft, sold or helped to sell drugs, attacked someone with the intent of hurting them or got into a serious fight in the past year.

In addition to crime data, the survey included information on important risk factors that researchers say are closely correlated with criminal involvement. They included whether the respondent had been a victim of a crime as a youth, various measures of family attachment as well as performance and attachment to school, whether the respondent had delinquent peers, lived in a neighborhood with gangs, or whether any of the respondent's peers were gang members.

Then Bersani compared second-generation immigrants with other native-born groups. She found that the results supported her theory that "their involvement in crime is the result of the same factors that explain involvement in crime among typical native-born youth."

For example, having peers in a gang increased the probability that an individual had been arrested in the previous year by 23% for second-generation immigrants and 25% for native-born non-Hispanic whites, Bersani wrote in an email. Similarly, having delinquent peers increases the likelihood of criminal or delinquent behavior by 6% for both groups. (The pattern was more mixed between second-generation immigrants and native-born blacks and Hispanics.)

This similar offending "profile" is strong evidence, she argues, that the generation crime gap among immigrants is due to the second-generation behaving like their native-born peers and not only as a consequence of growing up in two colliding worlds.

"Second generation immigrants appear to be catching-up to and resemble the typical native-born (white) population, at least in regard to their offending profile," she wrote. These findings "suggest that the children of immigrants seemingly fall prey to criminogenic influences in similar ways that native-born youth do."

1. The media often link immigration with increased crime, although studies show that first-generation immigrants actually have less criminal involvement than native-born Americans. According to the article, why might second-generation immigrants have more criminal involvement than their parents, thus fitting in with crime statistics in the typical native-born population?

"Q&A: CAN A DIVIDED EUROPE HANDLE THE REFUGEE CRISIS?" BY SEBASTIAN ROTELLA, FROM *PROPUBLICA*, SEPTEMBER 14, 2015

DEATHS AT SEA AND A CHAOTIC REFUGEE INFLUX REFLECT THE FAILURE OF EUROPEAN UNION LEADERS TO SETTLE ON A COMMON IMMIGRATION POLICY, ONE OF ITALY'S TOP ELECTED OFFICIALS TELLS *PROPUBLICA*.

Laura Boldrini, the president of Italy's Chamber of Deputies, has unusually strong credentials to discuss the immigration crisis gripping Europe. She worked for a quarter century at United Nations humanitarian agencies, serving as spokeswoman in southern Europe for the U.N. High Commission on Refugees.

Boldrini, 54, saw global migration at the front lines: the Italian island of Lampedusa, where seagoing migrants and refugees wash up, dead and alive, on the tides of despair and poverty; the refugee centers in Sicily where human traffickers exploit teenage Nigerian girls forced into prostitution; and the Greek coasts that are beach-heads for an unprecedented wave of refugees from Syria and Afghanistan.

In 2013, she was elected to Italy's Parliament as a candidate of today's governing center-left coalition. Two days after she took office, she was catapulted into the presidency of lower house of the Legislature, the eqauivalent of the U.S. Speaker of the House of Representatives.

Boldrini recently was in New York City and spoke with ProPublica about the immigration drama. European Union leaders have since moved closer to approving a plan to accept 160,000 refugees, though many see it as insufficient. This interview has been translated from Italian and edited for brevity.

Q. What are the roots of Europe's immigration crisis and what are the solutions?

I am not surprised that these migratory flows have increased. Last year, we attained the terrible record of 60 million refugees in the world, the highest number since World War II, because conflicts have increased. Sadly, solutions are not in sight. There is intense donor fatigue, which reduces the level of aid in the refugee camps, and this pushes people to travel further and risk their lives. There are protracted crises such as Syria. In the refugee camps, whoever has some savings left decides to attempt the big leap. We have to understand that during these past five years, nations such as Turkey, Jordan and Lebanon have accepted millions of refugees in their nations.

Immigration is the offspring of unresolved crises, the first collateral effect and the most visible one. In Europe, we are surrounded by instability. We have a nation like Libya a hundred miles away from us. A nation divided with a government in Tobruk, another in Tripoli, and then the tribes. We also have Syria, Iraq, the Horn of Africa. Somalia, still a hostage to al-Shabaab (the Islamic terrorist group). Eritrea, which has a dictator named Afwerki who forces young men and women to do indefinite military service and does not permit any freedom of expression.

Europe right now is not succeeding in responding to the challenges it confronts. We have to take advantage of this moment of difficulty and the opportunity it presents. In 70 years we have done a lot to construct our European identity. In a short time, we have undertaken an extraordinary journey. We have freedom of movement. When I was a girl, there were internal European borders. Our young people can study in any country. We have judicial cooperation. So this is positive, but it is no longer enough.

Now we have gone halfway, we have reached a ford in the river. Because today without a strong Europe, we don't count for anything compared to the rising global giants. We have to cross the ford and restart the motor of European integration, a motor that has stopped. But that means we have to give up something. We have to give up power to the European institutions. We have to share sovereignty. We need a single economic policy. A single European industrial policy. And an immigration policy.

It's not possible that only Italy and Greece receive migrants and that Germany is the only place where people go to request asylum. Or Sweden. If we are a union, we have to cooperate.

Q. What are some concrete responses to the migration crisis that Europe should implement?

We have to develop a coordinated asylum system. And have the same standard in all countries: European teams that manage the asylum issue. The same thing in Greece as in Norway as in Sweden as in other nations. If an Eritrean comes and asks me for asylum in Italy, he gets the same treatment as he would in Sweden. Today, on the other hand, if the same person requests asylum in one country he gets a certain response; if that person makes the request in another country, he gets a different response. So it's clear that they all want to go where they have the best chance of getting asylum. This leads to asylum-shopping in the EU.

We have to act on several levels. We have to continue to save human lives at sea. Not everyone agrees with this. But it's inhuman to think that if you have a passport, you get saved, and if you don't, you drown. But there are people who say that. I am proud that my country has taken the lead on this issue. We did Mare Nostrum (an Italian rescue operation in the Mediterranean) alone for a year at a cost of 9 million euros a month. Then it became European. Today we have Operation Triton.

Next: How do we reduce the number of people who risk human life at sea? We have to give an alternative, because if people know there is an alternative they won't risk their lives. The most concrete idea is to act in transit countries with a certain level of stability. You could create centers where international agencies do work – which, in fact, they are doing now, but with very limited resources. They do the screening of asylum requests and then offer quotas to nations that adhere to the program. You can do this in Tunisia, Egypt. It could be done by EU offices, not just UNHCR.

Q. Today's Islamic terrorists are less likely to arrive by sea as illegal immigrants than they are to be born in Paris or London or Rome. But there is at least some risk of bad people taking advantage of the chaotic immigration flows to reach Europe. Can Europe absorb and integrate so many people from war-torn Muslim countries?

We can't lower our guard. We have to be alert. We have to know who these people are. Of course, often they don't have documents. So you have to work with fingerprints. I also would say that if you want to carry out a terrorist act, you don't want to risk not making it. You want to be certain that you will arrive in Europe, and you can't have that certainty if you try to come illegally by sea.

As for the second point you raise – radicalization – that is one of the most serious problems. And it gets worse if people are excluded. If they are made to feel that they don't belong to a community. So I think we have to invest great effort and resources in policies of social inclusion. Because if a youth doesn't have any future and feels excluded, cut-off, pushed aside, marginalized, he wants something to believe in. And there are these merchants of terror who peddle dreams.

Q. You call for a "United States of Europe" with stronger EU institutions and more political integration. But the climate in Europe seems to defy profound change. Is it really possible to reform the EU to make it more effective and cohesive on fronts such as immigration, security and justice?

How does the European system work now? The strongest entity is the European Council, which is comprised of heads of state. Decisions are made by heads of state and heads of governments, and each seeks to defend their own national interest. And therefore they are not dealing with how this reduces the power of the European institutions. Instead, they concern themselves with their own immediate consensus. They follow the poll results, the dictatorship of the opinion polls.

We can't abandon the European dream. This is the critical moment to push harder. If there is fear, those who want to destroy the dream will win.

Q: On the day you entered politics, you had an experience that was emblematic of Europe's crisis.

I decided to run for office in response to a request. It was a surprise. I was working in Greece. It was on a very rough day. I was in Athens at a center run by Medecins du Monde (Doctors of the World).

There was a long line of people at the medical center, but I noticed many of them were Greek (rather than immigrants). The director of the center told me yes, the number of Greeks continued to increase. The economic situation was so tough they couldn't go to the hospital because they had to buy medicines there, and they didn't have enough money. So already in 2013, the Greek crisis was manifesting itself.

And while I was talking to the director, a group of people arrived who were shouting. There was an African youth who was weeping desperately. We went outside and saw that this African youth's face was all bloody and swollen. He had been beaten up by an extremist group. In Greece, these far-right groups form gangs, and when they see a person of color, they beat them up to make an example of them. He was just walking by. This happened in broad daylight.

What affected me the most was what the victim's African friends said. They were saying, in French: "That's enough, put an end to it, what do you want? They beat you up, that's what happens in Greece. You're black, it's normal that people beat you up." There was an acceptance of this brutality.

That evening, I was writing about this incident on my blog for the La Repubblica newspaper when Nichi Vendola called. (Vendola was the President of the Puglia region at the time and leader of the Left Ecology Liberty party.) I didn't know what he wanted. I burst out talking and told him about the whole horrible day. Then he said: "In fact, you have prepared the terrain for me. Today we are experiencing this situation in the entire Mediterranean. We want to give a new emphasis to the issue of rights. And since that's what you have always worked on during these years, we want to present you as a candidate for political office."

I told myself: I've worked for 25 years for the U.N. I have seen so many humanitarian crises in the world, from the Balkans to Afghanistan to Sudan. Pakistan. Iraq. I have seen the best and worst of the human race. Today, I have the possibility of doing something with all this experience, of using it in my country at the time when my country is living a difficult moment.

1. Laura Boldrini states that the European countries must unite in their response to the current global refugee crisis. Do you think the United States must become involved as well? In your opinion, what is the role of the United States in this global crisis?

"UNHCR VIEWPOINT: 'REFUGEE' OR 'MIGRANT' – WHICH IS RIGHT?" BY ADRIAN EDWARDS, FROM THE UN REFUGEE AGENCY, AUGUST 27, 2015

GENEVA, Aug 27 (UNHCR) – With almost 60 million people forcibly displaced globally and boat crossings of the Mediterranean in the headlines almost daily, it is becoming increasingly common to see the terms 'refugee' and 'migrant' being used interchangeably in media and public discourse. But is there a difference between the two, and does it matter?

Yes, there is a difference, and it does matter. The two terms have distinct and different meanings, and confusing them leads to problems for both populations. Here's why:

Refugees are persons fleeing armed conflict or persecution. There were 19.5 million of them worldwide at the end of 2014. Their situation is often so perilous and intolerable that they cross national borders to seek safety in nearby countries, and thus become internationally recognized as "refugees" with access to assistance from States, UNHCR, and other organizations. They are so recognized precisely because it is too dangerous for them to return home, and they need sanctuary elsewhere. These are people for whom denial of asylum has potentially deadly consequences.

Refugees are defined and protected in international law. The 1951 Refugee Convention and its 1967 Protocol as well as other legal texts, such as the 1969 OAU Refugee Convention, remain the cornerstone of modern refugee protection. The legal principles they enshrine have permeated into countless other international, regional, and national laws and practices. The 1951 Convention defines who is a refugee and outlines the basic rights which States should afford to refugees. One of the most fundamental principles laid down in international law is that refugees should not be expelled or returned to situations where their life and freedom would be under threat.

The protection of refugees has many aspects. These include safety from being returned to the dangers they have fled; access to asylum procedures that are fair and efficient; and measures to ensure that their basic human rights are respected to allow them to live in dignity and safety while helping them to find a longer-term solution. States bear the primary responsibility for this protection. UNHCR therefore works closely with governments, advising and supporting them as needed to implement their responsibilities.

Migrants choose to move not because of a direct threat of persecution or death, but mainly to improve their lives by finding work, or in some cases for education, family reunion, or other reasons. Unlike refugees who cannot safely return home, migrants face no such impediment to return. If they choose to return home, they will continue to receive the protection of their government.

For individual governments, this distinction is important. Countries deal with migrants under their own immigration laws and processes. Countries deal with refugees through norms of refugee protection and asylum that are defined in both national legislation and international law. Countries have specific responsibilities towards anyone seeking asylum on their territories or at their borders. UNHCR helps countries deal with their asylum and refugee protection responsibilities.

Politics has a way of intervening in such debates. Conflating refugees and migrants can have serious consequences for the lives and safety of refugees. Blurring the two terms takes attention away from the specific legal protections refugees require. It can undermine public support for refugees and the institution of asylum at a time when more refugees need such protection than ever before. We need to treat all human beings with respect and dignity. We need to ensure that the human rights of migrants are respected. At the same time, we also need to provide an appropriate legal response for refugees, because of their particular predicament.

So, back to Europe and the large numbers of people arriving this year and last year by boats in Greece, Italy and elsewhere. Which are they? Refugees or migrants?

In fact, they happen to be both. The majority of people arriving this year in Italy and Greece especially have been from countries mired in war or which otherwise are considered to be 'refugee-producing' and for whom international protection is needed. However, a smaller proportion is from elsewhere, and for many of these individuals, the term 'migrant' would be correct.

So, at UNHCR we say 'refugees and migrants' when referring to movements of people by sea or in other circumstances where we think both groups may be present – boat movements in Southeast Asia are another example. We say 'refugees' when we mean people fleeing war or persecution across an international border. And we say 'migrants' when we mean people moving for reasons not included in the legal definition of a refugee. We hope that others will give thought to doing the same. Choices about words do matter.

1. According to this article, what is the main difference between refugees and migrants?

2. Why is it important to distinguish between these two groups?

WHAT THE GOVERNMENT AND POLITICIANS SAY

Chapter 2 begins with a transcript of President Obama's 2015 address on immigration in which he lays out a plan for executive action that would enable some undocumented immigrants who meet specific criteria to remain in the country without fear of deportation. Obama acknowledges the dynamic benefits immigrants bring to the country but on several occasions asks immigrants to "get right with the law" if they wish to remain in the United States. Practically speaking, the president's "common-sense" approach masks some potentially troubling issues. For example, might those detained for minor offenses such as traffic infractions or marijuana possession end up deported as criminals? It is fair to wonder how Obama's executive order would play out in practice—if the courts uphold it.

Obama's executive order followed multiple failures to pass what has colloquially become known as the DREAM Act. The act (an acronym meaning Development, Relief, and Education for Alien Minors) would allow children meeting certain conditions and born in the United States to remain in the country, regardless of their parents' immigration status. In the second article of this chapter, John-Michael Rivera argues that questions about how (or if) to incorporate Mexican-American subjects have persisted since the United States annexed former Mexican lands in the nineteenth century. The author thus supplies important context to questions about the Mexican-American political subject, questions that are too often presented ahistorically.

The final two articles of the chapter address how members of the US Congress treat issues related to immigration and refugees. Terrorist attacks and the 2016 presidential election significantly impacted political discourse at the time of their writing.

"REMARKS BY THE PRESIDENT IN ADDRESS TO THE NATION ON IMMIGRATION," BY PRESIDENT BARACK OBAMA, FROM THE WHITE HOUSE, NOVEMBER 20, 2014

My fellow Americans, tonight, I'd like to talk with you about immigration.

For more than 200 years, our tradition of welcoming immigrants from around the world has given us a tremendous advantage over other nations. It's kept us youthful, dynamic, and entrepreneurial. It has shaped our character as a people with limitless possibilities—people not trapped by our past, but able to remake ourselves as we choose.

But today, our immigration system is broken—and everybody knows it.

Families who enter our country the right way and play by the rules watch others flout the rules. Business owners who offer their workers good wages and benefits see the competition exploit undocumented immigrants by paying them far less. All of us take offense to anyone who reaps the rewards of living in America without taking on the responsibilities of living in America. And undocumented immigrants who desperately want to embrace those responsibilities see little option but to remain in the shadows, or risk their families being torn apart.

It's been this way for decades. And for decades, we haven't done much about it.

When I took office, I committed to fixing this broken immigration system. And I began by doing what I could to secure our borders. Today, we have more agents and technology deployed to secure our southern border than at any time in our history. And over the past six years, illegal border crossings have been cut by more than half. Although this summer, there was a brief spike in unaccompanied children being apprehended at our border, the number of such children is now actually lower than it's been in nearly two years. Overall, the number of people trying to cross our border illegally is at its lowest level since the 1970s. Those are the facts.

Meanwhile, I worked with Congress on a comprehensive fix, and last year, 68 Democrats, Republicans, and Independents came together to pass a bipartisan bill in the Senate. It wasn't perfect. It was a compromise, but it reflected common sense. It would have doubled the number of border patrol agents, while giving undocumented immigrants a pathway to citizenship if they paid a fine, started paying their taxes, and went to the back of the line. And independent experts said that it would help grow our economy and shrink our deficits.

Had the House of Representatives allowed that kind of a bill a simple yes-or-no vote, it would have passed with support from both parties, and today it would be the law. But for a year and a half now, Republican leaders in the House have refused to allow that simple vote.

Now, I continue to believe that the best way to solve this problem is by working together to pass that kind of common sense law. But until that happens, there are actions I have the legal authority to take as President—the same kinds of actions taken by Democratic and Republican Presidents before me—that will help make our immigration system more fair and more just.

Tonight, I am announcing those actions.

First, we'll build on our progress at the border with additional resources for our law enforcement personnel so that they can stem the flow of illegal crossings, and speed the return of those who do cross over.

Second, I will make it easier and faster for high-skilled immigrants, graduates, and entrepreneurs to stay and contribute to our economy, as so many business leaders have proposed.

Third, we'll take steps to deal responsibly with the millions of undocumented immigrants who already live in our country.

I want to say more about this third issue, because it generates the most passion and controversy. Even as we are a nation of immigrants, we are also a nation of laws. Undocumented workers broke our immigration laws, and I believe that they must be held accountable—especially those who may be dangerous. That's why, over the past six years, deportations of criminals are up 80 percent. And that's why we're going to keep focusing enforcement resources on actual threats to our security. Felons, not families. Criminals, not children. Gang members, not a mother who's working hard to provide for her kids. We'll prioritize, just like law enforcement does every day.

But even as we focus on deporting criminals, the fact is, millions of immigrants—in every state, of every race and nationality—will still live here illegally. And let's be honest—tracking down, rounding up, and deporting millions of people isn't realistic. Anyone who suggests otherwise isn't being straight with you. It's also not who we are as Americans. After all, most of these immigrants have been here a long time. They work hard, often in tough, low-paying jobs. They support their families. They worship at our churches. Many of their kids are American-born or spent most of their lives here, and their hopes, dreams, and patriotism are just like ours. As my predecessor, President Bush, once put it: "They are a part of American life."

Now here's the thing: we expect people who live in this country to play by the rules. We expect that those who cut the line will not be unfairly rewarded. So we're going to offer the following deal: If you've been in America for more than five years; if you have children who are American citizens or legal residents; if you register, pass a criminal background check, and you're willing to pay your fair share of taxes—you'll be able to apply to stay in this country temporarily, without fear of deportation. You can come out of the shadows and get right with the law. That's what this deal is.

Now let's be clear about what it isn't. This deal does not apply to anyone who has come to this country recently. It does not apply to anyone who might come to America illegally in the future. It does not grant citizenship, or the right to stay here permanently, or offer the same benefits that citizens receive—only Congress can do that. All we're saying is we're not going to deport you.

I know some of the critics of this action call it amnesty. Well, it's not. Amnesty is the immigration system we have today—millions of people who live here without paying their taxes or playing by the rules, while politicians use the issue to scare people and whip up votes at election time. That's the real amnesty—leaving this broken system the way it is. Mass amnesty would be unfair. Mass deportation would be both impossible and contrary to our character. What I'm describing is accountability—a commonsense, middle ground approach: If you meet the criteria, you can come out of the shadows and get right with the law. If you're a criminal, you'll be deported. If you plan to enter the U.S. illegally, your chances of getting caught and sent back just went up.

The actions I'm taking are not only lawful, they're the kinds of actions taken by every single Republican President and every single Democratic President for the past half century. And to those Members of Congress who question my authority to make our immigration system work better, or question the wisdom of me acting where Congress has failed, I have one answer: Pass a bill.

I want to work with both parties to pass a more permanent legislative solution. And the day I sign that bill into law, the actions I take will no longer be necessary. Meanwhile, don't let a disagreement over a single issue be a dealbreaker on every issue. That's not how our democracy works, and Congress certainly shouldn't shut down our government again just because we disagree on this. Americans are tired of gridlock. What our country needs from us right now is a common purpose—a higher purpose.

Most Americans support the types of reforms I've talked about tonight. But I understand the disagreements held by many of you at home. Millions of us, myself included, go back generations in this country, with ancestors who put in the painstaking work to become citizens. So we don't like the notion that anyone might get a free pass to American citizenship.

I know some worry immigration will change the very fabric of who we are, or take our jobs, or stick it to middle-class families at a time when they already feel like they've gotten the raw end of the deal for over a decade. I hear these concerns. But that's not what these steps would do. Our history and the facts show that immigrants are a net plus for our economy and our society. And I believe it's important that all of us have this debate without impugning each other's character. Because for all the back-and-forth of Washington, we have to remember that this debate is about something bigger. It's about who we are as a country, and who we want to be for future generations.

Are we a nation that tolerates the hypocrisy of a system where workers who pick our fruit and make our beds never have a chance to get right with the law? Or are we a nation that gives them a chance to make amends, take responsibility, and give their kids a better future? Are we a nation that accepts the cruelty of ripping children from their parents' arms? Or are we a nation that values families, and works to keep them together?

Are we a nation that educates the world's best and brightest in our universities, only to send them home to create businesses in countries that compete against us? Or are we a nation that encourages them to stay and create jobs, businesses, and industries right here in America?

That's what this debate is all about. We need more than politics as usual when it comes to immigration; we need reasoned, thoughtful, compassionate debate that focuses on our hopes, not our fears. I know the politics of this issue are tough. But let me tell you why I have come to feel so strongly about it.

Over the past few years, I have seen the determination of immigrant fathers who worked two or three jobs, without taking a dime from the government, and at risk at any moment of losing it all, just to build a better life for their kids. I've seen the heartbreak and anxiety of children whose mothers might be taken away from them just because they didn't have the right papers. I've seen the courage of students who, except for the circumstances of their birth, are as American as Malia or Sasha; students who bravely come out as undocumented in hopes they could make a difference in a country they love.

These people—our neighbors, our classmates, our friends—they did not come here in search of a free ride or an easy life. They came to work, and study, and serve in our military, and above all, contribute to America's success.

Tomorrow, I'll travel to Las Vegas and meet with some of these students, including a young woman named Astrid Silva. Astrid was brought to America when she was four years old. Her only possessions were a cross, her doll, and the frilly dress she had on. When she started school, she didn't speak any English. She caught up to the other kids by reading newspapers and watching PBS, and became a good student. Her father worked in landscaping. Her mother cleaned other people's homes. They wouldn't let Astrid apply to a technology magnet school for fear the paperwork would out her as an undocumented immigrant—so she applied behind their back and got in. Still, she mostly lived in the shadows—until her grandmother, who visited every year from Mexico, passed away, and she couldn't travel to the funeral without risk of being found out and deported. It was around that time she decided to begin advocating for herself and others like her, and today, Astrid Silva is a college student working on her third degree.

Are we a nation that kicks out a striving, hopeful immigrant like Astrid—or are we a nation that finds a way to welcome her in? Scripture tells us that we shall not oppress a stranger, for we know the heart of a stranger—we were strangers once, too.

My fellow Americans, we are and always will be a nation of immigrants. We were strangers once, too. And whether our forebears were strangers who crossed the Atlantic, or the Pacific, or the Rio Grande, we are here only because this country welcomed them in, and taught them that to be an American is about something more than what we look like, or what our last names are, or how we worship. What makes us Americans is our shared commitment to an ideal—that all of us are created equal, and all of us have the chance to make of our lives what we will.

That's the country our parents and grandparents and generations before them built for us. That's the tradition we must uphold. That's the legacy we must leave for those who are yet to come.

Thank you, God bless you, and God bless this country we love.

1. Do you think Obama leans too heavily on the distinction between "criminals" and ordinary people, a distinction that might not be enforced fairly?

2. What factors might prevent undocumented migrants from "getting right with the law"? For example, an undocumented worker in the United States for five years or more could easily owe tens of thousands in back taxes. Is such a policy inherently class-based? Is this a problem, in your opinion, or merely a "responsibility" required of those living in the United States?

"THE DREAM ACT AND OTHER MEXICAN (AMERICAN) QUESTIONS," BY JOHN-MICHAEL RIVERA, FROM *PHI KAPPA PHI FORUM*, VOLUME 93, NUMBER 2, SUMMER 2013

This essay delves into some of the components that constitute Latino personhood in the United States. Most examples pertain to Mexican-Americans, who comprise the majority of the nation's 50 million Latinos, a cumulative demographic totaling about one-sixth of the 308-plus million people across the land. (1) Thus, the topic of Latino personhood encompasses vital concerns such as citizenship, belonging, inclusion, equality, and rights.

Because these issues remain a flash-point in immigration reform, I explore the ever-evolving and much-contested Development, Relief, and Education for Alien Minors (DREAM) Act. To unearth its rhetorical grounds, I must dig up roots buried deep in the dirt of America's soil. For queries about the DREAM Act come tethered to the U.S.'s expansionist past: fixed to the national subconscious but unmoored in the public desire to repress the relationship between immigration policies and pioneering precedents.

Here, then, this Latino perspective on tenets of the American dream—a social ideal stressing egalitarianism, freedom, happiness, and prosperity—incorporates acts of selective remembering and forgetting.

WELL-INTENTIONED DREAMS

On April 25, 2001, U.S. Rep. Luis Gutierrez, a Democrat from Illinois, was the first elected official to sponsor a federal version of what would become the DREAM Act. Then titled the Immigrant Children's Educational Advancement and Dropout Prevention Act, it attempted to help approximately 1.8 million undocumented immigrant students apply for permanent residency and legal citizenship. (2) The bill intended 1) "to provide an opportunity to certain alien children who were brought to the United States at a young age and have since been acculturated in the United States to adjust their status to lawful permanent residency and become contributing members of United States society," 2) "to restore to each state the flexibility to provide instate tuition to all children residing in the state, including to undocumented alien children," and 3) "to permit and encourage alien children who were brought to the United States at a young age and have been educated in United States elementary and secondary schools to continue their education through high school graduation and into college." (3) The bill spelled out age, residency, and educational requirements. It also stipulated that an applicant be "a person of good moral character."

A similar DREAM Act took shape a few months later. It was introduced in the Senate by Sen. Orrin Hatch of Utah, a Republican, and Sen. Richard Durbin of Illinois, a Democrat, and in the House of Representatives by Rep. Howard Berman of California, a Democrat, and Rep. Chris Cannon of Utah, a Republican. Additional key criteria specified that applicants be between the ages of 12 and 35 at the time of the bill's enactment; enter the country by age 15 or younger; prove five years of 1 continuous residence in the U.S. prior to the bill's enactment; have earned a G.E.D. or high school diploma; be younger than age 30 (though some subsequent bills extended this to age 35); and that males register for the Selective Service System. Other iterations followed on the state and federal levels. Recent federal and state bills have included the provision of enlisting in the armed forces (even though the military does not allow illegal aliens to enlist) (4) or acquiring a degree in higher education.

None of the numerous DREAM Acts became federal law (5) (though some states have passed renditions). One bill came up for a vote in the Senate in 2007, when it garnered 52 yeses, and another in 2010, when it managed 55, but neither reached the mandatory 60. The DREAM Act has been hotly debated, and all camps raise important agenda. The purpose of this essay is not to take sides (though I support the DREAM Act in principle). Rather, I want to point out rhetorical bases of the divisiveness and trace how this contemporary inquiry echoes a historical one. My contention is that the DREAM Act has gone through so many revisions and foments such dissent partly because of what happened when the U.S. took over more than half of Mexico in the mid-1800s; in other words, a mestizo past clouds contemporary race relations in the U.S. and the county's very concept of citizenship.

RHETORICAL DREAMS

Politicians who attack the DREAM Act note macro and micro problems. Some contend it translates to de facto amnesty for people crossing sovereign borders without permission. Sen. Jeff Sessions of Alabama, a Republican, declared in his 10 reasons to reject the DREAM Act that "this bill simply incentivizes and rewards more illegality" for immigrants who practice "unacceptable lawlessness." (6) Other officeholders assert the DREAM Act would import cheap labor and cause hardships for states and schools because of the influx of new citizens. "I can't endorse [it] because there is a lot of money involved," said former Rep. Ron Paul of Texas, a Libertarian. "And you know there are a lot of subsidies in there between the billions of dollars." (7) Pat McDonough, a Republican in the Maryland House of Delegates, tallied "the burden on the citizen taxpayer" of the DREAM Act. "Let us put aside emotional misinformation and whip out our calculators." His math: Maryland taxpayers would underwrite hundreds of millions of dollars annually "to educate people who cannot legally work in this state or country.

And because most DREAM Act students will not have to pay out-of-state tuition and will displace those who do, "This loss must be replaced by the taxpayers, tuition increases, or reduced spending." (8) Objectors also mention ethics. When Gov. Jerry Brown of Calif., a Democrat, granted illegal immigrants the same access as state residents to financial aid at higher education public campuses, Calif. Assemblyman Tim Donnelly, a Republican, decried, "It's morally wrong. We have just created a new entitlement that is going to cause tens of thousands of people to come here illegally from all over the world." (9) And one naysayer tried to ground logic in quality control and took on racial overtones. Iowa Rep. Steve King, a Republican, compared allowing some people to immigrate to choosing among canines, implying that good moral character came down to breeding and training. "You want a good bird dog? You want one that's going to be aggressive?" he analogized. "Pick the one that's the friskiest, the one that's engaged the most and not the one that's over there sleeping in the corner." (10)

Politicians who favor the DREAM Act also cite the forest and the trees regarding the economic, social, and cultural development of the U.S. In April 2011, 22 Democratic senators collectively wrote President Barack Obama: "We strongly believe that DREAM Act students should not be removed from the United States, because they have great potential to contribute to our country and children should not be punished for their parents' mistakes." The petitioners quote Obama: "As you said in your [2011] State of the Union Address, 'let's stop expelling talented, responsible young people who could be staffing our research labs or starting a new business, who could be further enriching this nation." The letter ends: "We look forward to working with you on ways we can enable this talented group of young people to contribute to this nation they call home." (11)

Sen. Durbin created a page on his website (12) that echoes that letter. The page also references a UCLA study indicating that DREAM Act beneficiaries could contribute $1.4 trillion to $3.6 trillion to the U.S. economy over 40 years. (13) The page further alludes to American values by compiling "DREAMers' stories" from affected parties—disparate voices in the chorus that is America—and by inferring that majority rules through the assertion that the DREAM Act is "supported by labor, business, education, civil rights and religious groups" and "has broad bipartisan support in Congress and from the American people." Along these lines, the official statement by "deeply disappointed" Sen. Dianne Feinstein of California, a Democrat, after the 2010 DREAM Act failed to pass the Senate also appealed to red, white and blue precepts, plus conscience and guilt: "Many of these young people grew up in the United States and have little or no memory or resources of the country from which they came. They are hard-working young people dedicated to their education or serving in the nation's military. They have stayed out of trouble. Some are valedictorians. I happen to know one. And some are honor roll students. Some are community leaders, and have an unwavering commitment to serving the United States of America." (14)

Unsurprisingly, the DREAM Act became a touchstone in Obama's 2012 reelection campaign against Republican presidential candidate Mitt Romney. For example, in a speech last September to Latino voters, Obama, a Democrat, reminded nationwide listeners that he had backed it. (15) This outreach reinforced a May 2012 speech Obama made at a Cinco de Mayo celebration in the White House Rose Garden about how "securing our future depends on making sure that all Americans have the opportunity to reach their potential....And it is long past the time that we unleash the promise of all our young people and make the DREAM Act a reality....I want to sign the DREAM Act into law ... making sure that our sons and daughters have every opportunity to realize the American dream." (16)

Shortly thereafter, Obama signed a quick fix to get around some persistent roadblocks. The executive order Consideration of Deferred Action for Childhood Arrivals allows those who entered the country illegally as minors, who are younger than age 31, who have lived in the U.S. for at least five consecutive years, and who pose no threat to national security or public safety, among other rules, to remain without fear of deportation. "While this process does not provide lawful status or a pathway to permanent residence or citizenship, individuals whose cases are deferred will not be removed from the United States for a two-year period, subject to renewal, and may also receive employment authorization," according to the Department of Homeland Security and the U.S. Citizenship and Immigration Services." (17) Obama termed this a "temporary stopgap measure" to "mend our nation's immigration policy, to make it more fair, more efficient, and more just—specifically for certain young people sometimes called 'Dreamers." He added that "it makes no sense to expel talented young people, who, for all intents and purposes, are Americans..." (18)

HISTORICAL DREAMS

As many as 1.7 million of the 4.4 million unauthorized immigrants age 30 and younger may qualify for this deferral, and 85 percent of the former are Hispanic, estimates the nonpartisan Pew Hispanic Center. (19) (There are 11.2 million unauthorized immigrants collectively in the U.S. (20) The U.S. Immigration and Customs Enforcement agency "removed" 409,849 in fiscal year 2012. (21)) And media outlets like CNN reported that Consideration of Deferred Action for Childhood Arrivals is "one of the biggest immigration policy changes in years." (22)

Nevertheless, the DREAM Act, like a literal dream, never seems to realize itself and federal legislation remains in limbo until the next sleep or news cycle. In fact, the ongoing dispute is part of a historical—and historic—public discussion about Latinos in the U.S. Although Obama's Cinco de Mayo speech probably doesn't suggest the treatment of Latinos in the 19th century, specifically the Treaty of Guadalupe Hidalgo of 1847-48, his sensibility nonetheless brings to mind this formal agreement that ended the U.S.-Mexico War of 1846-48.

The main spark to ignite the war flared in 1836 when Texas declared its independence from Mexico. Complex geopolitical and economic disagreements between the U.S., which would annex the Republic of Texas in 1845, and Mexico further inflamed matters. (23) The treaty, signed on Feb. 2, 1848, under the administration of U.S. President James K. Polk and Mexican representatives Don Bernardo Couto, Don Miguel Atristain and Don Luis Gonzaga Cuevas, was the first document to deal with the U.S. capacity to expand to the West and with the newly constituted political subject of the Mexican-American. Articles 5 and 8-11 (though 10 was ultimately omitted) and parts of 12 granted Mexicans the legal right to be included, by choice, in the body politic as "American citizens" and geographically defined and ceded 55 percent of all Mexican lands, some 525,000 square miles (present-day California, Texas, Arizona, and New Mexico and parts of Colorado, Nevada, Utah, Wyoming, and Oregon), to the U.S. in exchange for $15 million (Article 12). In some ways, then, the treaty wound up as a type of DREAM Act because this early accord stands as the initial official attempt to address the civil rights of Mexicans. (24)

Nevertheless, as Latin American studies expert Martha Menchaca, a professor at University of Texas at Austin, argues, the treaty only gave a semblance of democratic inclusion to Mexican-Americans because their mixed background "put them in an ambiguous position," she posits. They did not fit into the predominant understanding of U.S. citizenship requirements, which were Eurocentric. (25)

Indeed, comments from politicians from the era suggest this discrepancy. Social reformer and Scottish immigrant Robert Dale Owen, who held numerous offices in his career, considered the war and the treaty the most important aspects of U.S. national character. (26) Former U.S. vice president and multifarious public servant John C. Calhoun disagreed, denigrating Mexicans as "a motley amalgamation of impure races, not [even] as good as Cherokees or Choctaws," and disbelieving that American could "incorporate a people so dissimilar in every aspect—so little qualified for free and popular government—without certain destruction of our political institutions. We do not want the people of Mexico, either as citizens or subjects." (27)

The warrant of this general inquest echoes the prescient work of political journalist John L. O'Sullivan, perhaps best known for coining the term "Manifest Destiny," a belief that Americans were fated to expand across the continent, in 1845. O'Sullivan wrote a seminal essay that year called, in fact, "The Mexican Question." Published in *The United States Magazine and Democratic Review*, for which he was editor, it served as one of the first documents to explore the rights and status of Mexican inhabitants in regions annexed to the U.S. after the Texas independence movement of 1836. The complicated piece helped justify America's expansion but also revealed a rising scrutiny about America's ability to incorporate Mexican realms. One key passage states: "What then has become of the war between Texas and Mexico? Her war is as much at an end as in a litigation between individuals, the death of the one terminates it, as between those parties....By the Annexation, Mexico is brought up face to face with a new party, the United States." Sullivan emphatically concludes that Mexicans have no basis to complain about the U.S. expansion: "Away with this Mexican gasconading about her pretend rights and pretend wrongs!" (28)

In *The Emergence of Mexican America*, my 2006 book published by New York University Press, I explain how this ambiguity gave way to thousands of "Mexican questions" in the public sphere. (29) The powers that be needed to figure out the dynamics between the two countries, of course, but also the role of Mexicans in the U.S. in civics and in culture. These topics preoccupied writers on both sides of the border, including the Mexican and Texan statesman Lorenzo de Zavala, whose works, on both Mexico and the U.S., were read well after his death in 1836, and the American author Stephen Crane (who spent time in Mexico and the American West when employed as a journalist) in his short story, "A Man and Some Others," about an American cowboy and Mexicans on the border, published in *Century Magazine* in 1897. Indeed, hundreds of period pieces—newspapers, comics, books, essays, and political tracts—raised O'Sullivan's Mexican question and even tried to answer it. For instance, Charles E. Averill's 1847 dime novel *The Mexican Ranchero; or, The Maid of Chapparal* uses a romance to demonstrate that yes, Mexicans can be included as citizens through marriage. Maria Amparo Ruiz de Burton, the first female Mexican-American author to write novels in English, entitles a chapter of *The Squatter and the Don* (1885) about these affairs: "The Don's View of the Treaty." She bases that character, Don Mariano Alamar, on her good friend Mariano Vallejo, the California military commander, politician and rancher, and has him announce, "[T]ruly I believe that Congress itself did not anticipate the effect of its laws upon us and how we have been despoiled, we the conquered people." (30) And Karl Marx and Friedrich Engels speculated repeatedly about whether the "independence of a few Spanish Californians and Texans" could affect Communism. (31)

Thus, the Mexican question that emerged from O'Sullivan and the political arena and print culture of the 19th century set the rhetorical foundations for American and Mexicans relations for decades to come—and laid some building blocks for (Mexican) American dreams of citizenship in general and the DREAM Acts in particular.

FUTURE DREAMS

Pressing deliberations about immigrants—What is their status? What are their rights? What is their race? What is their economic impact? Will they assimilate? Should they assimilate?—continue to enhance American democracy's possibilities and expose its limitations. Of course, the political sphere is not the only venue to grapple with these questions today. From writer/director Sergio Arau's 2004 movie *A Day Without a Mexican* to the literary fiction of Junot Diaz to the murals of Judy Baca, leading lights in cultural spheres also ruminate on them.

One of the most compelling depictions, at least for me, comes from a political cartoon. This Rex F. May syndicated "Baloo" strip captures the tricky negotiations about immigrant rights and status and nails the central irony of the DREAM Act. This colorful panel subverts the fantastic dreams of alien abduction. Two arrivals from space, one pregnant, have traveled to Earth to stay and wonder if their unborn child will become an American citizen when the due day comes. (Interestingly, they do not ask about their own status as new members of the land.) Puzzled, the brown-suited everyman is speechless. I suspect the fellow ponders why they made the journey in the first place. And the intergalactic incomers do not extend him an invitation to fly off to their foreign home, either. Instead, he is confronted with a fundamental quandary that spans citizenship, belonging, inclusion, equality and rights, to which he has no answer.

Their simple inquiry about birthright, then, epitomizes and spoofs the controversy about aliens in the U.S.

and what to do about their children. Tackling this now is all the more urgent because the Hispanic population is expected to rise to more than 130 million, or one-third of the country's population, by 2050, according to the U.S. Census Bureau. (32)

What the U.S. will look like in the years and decades to come and how Latinos will be defined are themes that have moved to the forefront of public discourse. Indeed, last year the Census Bureau questioned if Hispanics should be deemed a racial category rather than an ethnicity. How do Latinos view their standing in the U.S.? How do "native" citizens view Latinos? The answers continue to unfold. As a result, so do the definitions of the American dream. The Hispanic voice in America remains as muffled as it is clear.

1. Obama has deported undocumented immigrants in record numbers, yet he has also championed legislation to prevent some deportations. What do you make of the ambiguity in his record?

2. How does the history the author points to regarding the Mexican-American War bear on the DREAM Act? Does he make this connection sufficiently clear?

"LETTER TO PRESIDENT OBAMA FROM THE COMMITTEE ON HOMELAND SECURITY," BY MICHAEL T. MCCAUL, CHAIRMAN OF THE COMMITTEE ON HOMELAND SECURITY, US HOUSE OF REPRESENTATIVES, JUNE 11, 2015

Dear President Obama,

A major consequence of the global surge in Islamist extremism has been the displacement of millions of people in war zones across the Middle East and North Africa. Your Administration has announced plans to resettle some of these refugees here in the United States. In a Committee on Homeland Security hearing held in February, the Director of the National Counterterrorism Center acknowledged that refugees from the conflict in Syria and Iraq being admitted to the United States were "a population of concern," given the possibility that members of the Islamic State of Iraq and Syria (ISIS) or al Qaeda networks such as al Nusra Front might attempt to exploit refugee programs to gain entry into the United States.

It is my understanding that the Department of State intends to admit 2,000 Syrian refugees this fiscal year and many more in 2016 and beyond, in addition to more than 500 admitted since 2011. While we have a proud history of welcoming refugees, the Syrian conflict is a unique case requiring heightened vigilance and scrutiny. It represents the single largest convergence of Islamist terrorists in history, including those associated with the Islamic State of Iraq and Syria (ISIS), al Qaeda, and Hezbollah.

We are increasingly concerned by the decision to accelerate the resettlement of thousands of Syrian refugees here in the United States despite the serious national security implications of doing so. There is a real risk that individuals associated with terrorist groups will attempt to exploit the refugee resettlement program in order to gain entry into our country. Terrorist networks are constantly probing our defenses and would not hesitate to manipulate a program meant to save those fleeing violence for the purpose of infiltrating operatives onto American soil. Indeed, ISIS's predecessor al Qaeda in Iraq (AQI) has already successfully exploited U.S. government refugee resettlement programs in 2009 when two terrorists responsible for killing four Pennsylvania National Guard soldiers in Iraq in 2005 were granted entry and resettled in Bowling Green, Kentucky.

Our screening processes currently suffer from vulnerabilities given the dynamic terrorist threat environment in Syria, the lack of intelligence sources on the ground, and the paucity of biometric and biographic information needed to conduct high-confidence assessments. As FBI's Assistant Director for Counterterrorism testified before the House Homeland Security Committee in February, due to the lack of a U.S. footprint on the ground in Syria "the databases won't have the information we need" for effective vetting. Simply put, we cannot screen against derogatory information we do not have.

My Committee and I have been sounding the alarm for months. I am deeply disappointed that your Administration failed to fully respond in a timely manner to our concrete requests on this important national security issue, including our February 19, 2015 letter from the Committee.

The United States has a national security interest in destroying the terrorist networks currently operating in Syria and Iraq, and in preventing groups such as al Qaeda and ISIS from carrying out attacks against the United States and our allies. While the refugee resettlement program represents the very best of the United States' generous and altruistic nature and is a necessary and valuable effort to provide assistance to some families devastated by conflict, we cannot allow terrorists who pose a direct threat to the U.S. Homeland to exploit these programs to carry out attacks on our soil.

Our outstanding questions have taken on greater urgency after ISIS demonstrated its ability to infiltrate and seize refugee camps in Syria earlier last month. I respectfully request that your Administration provide Members on the Committee of Homeland Security with a classified interagency briefing on these issues and a set of written responses from the Department of State and the FBI to the initial questions asked in February no later than July 7, 2015.

I am hopeful that your Administration will cooperate with my Committee in earnest so that we can help ensure the safety of the American people.

Sincerely,

Michael T. McCaul
Chairman

The Honorable Jeh Johnson
Secretary
U.S. Department of Homeland Security
Washington DC 20528

The Honorable Loretta E. Lynch
Attorney General
U.S. Department of Justice
950 Pennsylvania Avenue, NW
Washington, DC 20530

The Honorable James B. Comey
Director
Federal Bureau of Investigation
935 Pennsylvania Avenue, NW
Washington, DC 20535

Ms. Lisa Monaco
Assistant to the President for
Homeland Security and Counterterrorism
The White House
1600 Pennsylvania Avenue, NW
Washington, DC 20500

Mr. Nicholas J. Rasmussen
Director
The National Counterterrorism Center
Office of the Director of National Intelligence
Washington, DC 20511

1. Do you think this letter presents enough evidence that Syrian refugees could pose a security threat to the United States? What evidence is given?

"'WRONG SIDE OF HISTORY': OUTRAGE AS US CONGRESS MOVES TO BLOCK SYRIAN REFUGEES," BY SARAH LAZARE, FROM *COMMON DREAMS*, NOVEMBER 18, 2015

LAWMAKERS SPEW XENOPHOBIC RHETORIC JUST DAYS AFTER GOVERNORS LEVY THREATS TO KEEP OUT THOSE FLEEING WAR

The xenophobic rhetoric that erupted on the state level in the U.S. in the immediate wake of the Paris attacks is now taking the national stage, where Republicans and some Democrats in Congress are attempting to rush through legislation before the Thanksgiving recess that would block Syrians fleeing war from taking refuge in the United States.

The anti-Syrian hysteria among lawmakers has been criticized as racist, Islamophobic, and deeply inhumane—invoking the U.S. legacies of the Japanese internment camps and the Chinese Exclusion act.

In both the House and Senate this week, politicians are brazenly calling for a halt to President Barack Obama's stated plan to admit up to 10,000 additional Syrians—which has already been criticized as shamefully inadequate and cumbersome, particularly given the role of the United States in driving the crisis.

Newly-minted House Speaker Paul Ryan (R-Wis.) declared at a press conference on Tuesday that "we cannot allow terrorists to take advantage of our compassion. This is a moment where it is better to be safe than to be sorry. So we think the prudent, the responsible thing is to take a pause in this particular aspect of this refugee program in order to verify that terrorists are not trying to infiltrate the refugee population."

Ryan said he will ask the House to hold a vote on a bill to halt the program before the break.

Majority Leader Rep. Kevin McCarthy (R-Calif.), who leads the counter-terrorism task force, said Tuesday that the House will, indeed, vote Thursday on a piece of legislation spearheaded by Rep. Richard Hudson (R-N.C.) that would require such extensive FBI background checks that Syrians would be effectively barred from admittance to the country.

"The vetting process now in place is already a dreadful maze—a Rubik's Cube of bureaucracies practically guaranteeing that few Syrians will ever set foot on our shores," James Jennings, president of Conscience International, said in a press statement on Wednesday. "The process takes up to three years and requires 21 steps with numerous agencies, including the Department of Homeland Security, all required to sign off."

The push is not just a Republican effort. Sens. Charles Schumer (D-N.Y.) and Joe Manchin (D-W.Va.) have both called for Obama to shut out refugees.

Some politicians are not hiding their anti-Muslim motives. GOP presidential candidate Sen. Ted Cruz (Texas) told *Fox News* on Saturday that Syrian Muslim refugees should be sent to "majority-Muslim countries" instead of being welcomed to the United States. "On the other hand," he added, "Christians who are being targeted for genocide, for persecution, Christians who are being beheaded or crucified, we should be providing safe haven to them."

And on Sunday, 2016 Republican candidate Jeb Bush said, "I think our focus ought to be on the Christians who have no place in Syria anymore." When asked how he would identify Christian Syrians, Bush replied: "You're a Christian—I mean, you can prove you're a Christian. You can't prove it, then, you know, you err on the side of caution."

These comments come despite the fact that, as author and professor Laila Lalami wrote earlier this week, "Muslims are the primary victims of ISIS, and its primary resisters. It is an insult to every one of the hundreds of thousands of Muslim victims of terrorism to lump them with the lunatics who commit terror."

"Punishing Syrian refugees for crimes committed by violent extremists is the last thing we should be doing now," Raed Jarrar, government relations manager for the American Friends Service Committee, told *Common Dreams*. "Although the U.S. has played a negative role in creating the conditions that have led to the ongoing disasters in the Middle East region, it has not lived up to its responsibilities to end the conflicts or assist refugees."

Speaking from a trip in Manila, Obama declared Tuesday: "When candidates say we should not admit 3-year-old orphans, that's political posturing. When individuals say we should have religious tests, and only Christians, proven Christians, should be allowed, that's offensive and contrary to American values."

While rights groups are asking for far more refugees to be welcomed than Obama is calling for, many also argue that a defeat to his plan would be a major step backwards. At least 80 humanitarian, labor, and civil rights groups on Tuesday released an open letter to Congress expressing support for Obama's plan. "Syrian refugees are fleeing exactly the kind of terror that unfolded on the streets of Paris," stated the missive, whose signatories include the ACLU and Farmworker Justice.

While the anti-Syrian bills will likely fail in Congress, McConnell and Ryan could be setting up a government shutdown showdown if they tie the bill to the government spending legislation, *Vox* reporter Dara Lind noted on Wednesday.

Meanwhile, over half of U.S. governors vowed this week to ban Syrian refugees from their states. While Obama administration officials say that these governors do not have the legal grounding to impose such bans, their pledges nonetheless send the message to Syrians they are not welcome—and could contribute to further blowback.

Christine Neumann-Ortiz, executive director of the Wisconsin-based social justice group Voces de la Frontera, said Tuesday that the state's governor Scott Walker, in levying such a threat, "has placed himself on the same side of history as those who turned away Jewish refugees fleeing Europe and interned Japanese Americans and German Americans during World War II."

Meanwhile, rights campaigners argue that welcoming in Syrians is the least the U.S. can do.

"Resettling Syrian refugees to the U.S. is only one of the many tools that should be utilized to respond to the crisis of displaced Syrians," said Jarrar. "Helping displaced Syrians while they're still in Syria and the region is an even more important method to respond. A comprehensive solution to displacement will happen through a political solution in Syria that would allow for voluntary repatriation."

1. Imagine you are a legislator in the US Congress. Would you support a pause in Syrian immigration? Why or why not?

CHAPTER 3

WHAT THE COURTS AND LEGAL COMMUNITY SAY

W hat defines a refugee, legally speaking? In the precedent-setting case of *Immigration and Naturalization Service v. Elias-Zacarias* summarized below, the Supreme Court ruled that an asylum seeker must conclusively demonstrate that he or she is fleeing political persecution. Matthew H. Joseph articulates the practical challenges refugees face in accomplishing this. Since the burden of proof lies on the refugee, it is difficult to distinguish between a generalized threat and political coercion.

Further legal challenges began in 2010, as Arizona enacted legislation vesting local authorities with greatly increased power over immigration law and policy, including the right to request citizenship documentation during lawful stops. The Supreme

Court eventually reaffirmed federal control over immigration policy, ruling that three out of four sections of the Arizona law were pre-empted by federal law. However, the Supreme Court upheld Section 2, the controversial "show us your papers" provision that allows law enforcement to investigate the immigration status of any individual deemed "suspicious." This broadly expanded Arizona state police power and raised much concern over possible racial profiling.

While the federal government was unambiguous in ruling that Arizona could not construct its own immigration policy, state laws that require employers to verify an employee's citizenship status remained on the books. With Arizona's workaround successful, many worry that other states will take similar measures to restrict immigration. Civil rights and due process, it seems, may become collateral damage if such a repressive movement gains traction.

"IMMIGRATION AND NATURALIZATION SERVICE V. ELIAS-ZACARIAS: PARTIALLY CLOSING THE DOOR ON POLITICAL ASYLUM," BY MATTHEW H. JOSEPH, FROM *THE MARYLAND LAW REVIEW*, 1993

INTRODUCTION

In *Immigration and Naturalization Service v. Elias-Zacarias*, (I) the Supreme Court held that the United States government could legally deport an alien whose desire to remain neutral in his country's civil war had exposed him to threats of violence and forced conscription into a guerrilla army. (2) The Court found that the alien's neutrality did not constitute a "political opinion" for the purposes of protection under federal immigration law. (3) Therefore, the alien could not be considered a "refugee" eligible for political asylum in the United States. (4) This case marks a significant narrowing of the definition of "refugee" and will make it harder for applicants for political asylum to prove that they have suffered "persecution on account of...political opinion." The *Elias-Zacarias* Court also rejected the standard of review for administrative decision-making used by the majority of the courts of appeals in reviewing whether an alien can statutorily be considered a "refugee." (5) In so doing, the Court established a standard of review that closely approximates an abuse of discretion standard, effectively limiting the ability of the federal courts to oversee executive branch immigration policies. (6) *Elias-Zacarias* clearly marks a turning away from the Court's traditional reluctance to interpret immigration statutes in a way that results in the deportation of an alien with a questionable claim. (7)

This Note describes the status of federal immigration law regarding political asylum preceding the *Elias-Zacarias* decision. It then explores the Court's reasoning behind its decision in *Elias-Zacarias*. Finally, this Note concludes by considering the decision's potential impact on immigration policy and other areas of law.

I. STATEMENT OF THE CASE

Jairo Jonathan Elias-Zacarias fled his native Guatemala when he was eighteen years old, after two armed guerrillas threatened to force him to join their anti-government efforts. (8) The guerrillas, wearing uniforms and with handkerchiefs masking their identities, came to Elias-Zacarias's home and asked him to join their movement. (9) He refused "because the guerrillas were against the government and he was afraid that the government would retaliate against him and his family if he did join the guerrillas." (10) The guerrillas accepted his refusal but promised to return later. (11) He left two months after the guerrillas first appeared, (12) fearing that the guerrillas would "take [him] and kill [him]" if he refused them again. (13)

After being apprehended in July 1987 for "entering the United States without inspection," (14) Elias-Zacarias attempted to avoid deportation using two strategies authorized by federal immigration law: asylum and withholding of deportation. (15) While the asylum test is the easier of the two to meet, only withholding of deportation is nondiscretionary.

To gain political asylum under section 208 of the Immigration and Nationality Act (INA), aliens must show that they are refugees according to the statutory definition. Section 101 of the INA defines "refugee" as:

> any person who is outside any country of such person's nationality or, in the case of a person having no nationality, is outside any country in which such person last habitually resided, and who is unable or unwilling to return to, and is unable or unwilling to avail himself or herself of the protection of, that country because of persecution or a well-founded fear of persecution on account of race, religion, nationality, membership in a particular social group, or political opinion ....(16)

Even if an alien meets this standard, the government has discretion to refuse the refugee asylum. (17)

To gain a withholding of deportation, aliens must show that their "life or freedom would be threatened in such country on account of race, religion, nationality, membership in a particular social group, or political opinion. (18) If an alien meets this test, the government has no discretion because the statutory language is mandatory. (19) Aliens may not be deported to the country which poses the threat; however, they may be deported to another country where the risk is not present. (20)

Aliens applying for asylum or withholding of deportation are protected by certain due process requirements. Under the INA, aliens are entitled to a hearing before an immigration judge from the Immigration and Naturalization Service (INS). (21) They are also entitled to appeal the immigration judge's decision to the Board of Immigration Appeals (BIA or the Board) and, if necessary, to appeal the BIA ruling to a federal court of appeals. (22)

In *Elias-Zacarias*, the immigration judge denied the alien's application for asylum on the grounds that the guerrillas had neither threatened Elias-Zacarias nor returned to his home as they had promised. (23) At his appeal to the BIA, however, Elias-Zacarias produced a letter from his father that mentioned several return visits by the guerrillas. (24) Despite this new evidence, the Board held that Elias-Zacarias had not shown an objective basis for his fears. (25) It found that there was no evidence of a pattern of conscription on the part of the guerrillas in Guatemala. As a result, the Board affirmed the immigration judge's ruling. (26)

The Court of Appeals for the Ninth Circuit reversed the decision of the BIA, (27) finding that Elias-Zacarias had proven an objective basis of fear by establishing that there existed a pattern of forced conscription in his native land. (28) The court first determined that conscription of an unwilling person by a nongovernmental group was a form of persecution intended to be protected by the INA. (29) The Ninth Circuit then carefully reviewed the BIA's refusal to grant Elias-Zacarias refugee status and re-applied the federal requirements, this time to the alien's benefit. (30)

The Supreme Court granted certiorari (31) and reversed the decision of the Ninth Circuit by a six-to-three vote in a concise opinion by Justice Scalia. (32) Narrowly reading the language in section 208 requiring "persecution on account of . . .political opinion," the Court held that Elias-Zacarias' neutrality was not a "political opinion" and, therefore, he had not sufficiently demonstrated a "well-founded fear" of persecution due to a political opinion. (33) The Court also indicated that greater deference was to be accorded to the BIA decision than that given by the Ninth Circuit. (34) In his dissent, Justice Stevens, joined by Justices Blackmun and O'Connor, determined that Elias-Zacarias did possess a "well-founded fear" of persecution based upon his adoption of a neutral position in Guatemala's civil war. (35)

II. SUMMARY OF THE REASONING

In *Elias-Zacarias*, the Court first addressed the alien's argument that he was expressing a political opinion by refusing to join the guerrillas. (36) The Court rejected this proposition on two grounds. First, the Court argued that a person could wish to avoid forced conscription for any number of reasons, many of which were not political in nature. (37) Justice Scalia, writing for the majority, used Elias-Zacarias' own testimony-that his refusal to join the guerrillas was motivated by his fear of government retal-iation-to show that Elias-Zacarias was not attempting to make a political statement. (38) Second, the Court rejected the proposition that a decision to remain neutral was itself an "affirmative expression of a political opinion" intended to be protected from persecution. (39) Justice Scalia stated that this notion "seems to us not ordinarily so. (40)

The Court then rejected Elias-Zacarias' claim that threatened conscription constitutes "persecution" under the statute. The guerrillas' policy of forced recruitment, according to the majority, stemmed from a desire and need to fill their army with additional bodies rather than from any dissatisfaction with the political beliefs of the conscriptees. (41) The Court interpreted the "ordinary meaning" of the statute's language to require that the persecution be "on account of" the "*victim's* political opinions, not the persecutor's. (42) Thus, Elias-Zacarias failed to meet the standard. (43)

In so holding, the Court placed a heavy burden on the asylum seeker, indicating that Elias-Zacarias must show "compelling" evidence for reversal of the BIA decision. (44) That is, the Court required him to prove that the BIA's ruling was not "reasonable. (45) The Court quoted for emphasis the portion of the INA that requires a court of appeals to affirm a BIA decision that is "supported by reasonable, substantial and probative evidence on the record considered as whole." (46) In interpreting that language, the Court examined past cases and concluded that Elias-Zacarias could succeed "only if the evidence presented by Elias-Zacarias was such that a reasonable factfinder would have to conclude that the requisite fear of persecution existed." (47)

III. LEGAL CONTEXT

The two legal strategies used by Elias-Zacarias—seeking asylum and withholding of deportation—exist in statutory form in the Refugee Act of 1980 (Refugee Act). (48) The Refugee Act marked a major change in federal immigration law. Prior to its passage, withholding of deportation was subject to the discretion of the Attorney General. (49) The Refugee Act removed the Attorney General's discretion, making withholding of deportation mandatory for eligible aliens, (50) thereby bringing United States law into conformance with United Nations guidelines. (51) In addition, passage of the Refugee Act reflected a strong congressional intent to create a more systematic, consistent and humanitarian asylum policy. (52) Congress wanted to ensure that American immigration policy would no longer be determined on an ad hoc basis, which had resulted in both ideologically-slanted and arbitrary decisions. (53)

Despite passage of the Refugee Act, critics have charged that the United States government's asylum policy has remained biased and overly strict. The government has narrowly interpreted the refugee definition to exclude thousands of potential refugees. (54) For example, the Bush Administration found the thousands of Haitians fleeing their country during the last decade to be in search of "economic betterment, not political shelter." (55) This made deportation possible. The result in many cases has been that refugees from countries friendly with the United States have an exceedingly more difficult time obtaining asylum than those refugees from countries toward whom the United States is hostile. (56)

A. SUPREME COURT CLARIFICATIONS

The Refugee Act created many uncertainties that the courts have slowly clarified. For example, the Refugee Act did not define the standards of proof by which aliens must make their cases for asylum and withholding of deportation. (57) Section 243(h) mandates withholding of deportation when an "alien's life or freedom would be threatened." (58) In *Immigration and Naturalization Service v. Stevic*, (59) the Court found that the "would be threatened" language requires aliens to show a "clear probability" of a risk (60) and that the persecution was "more likely than not to occur." (61)

Section 101 of the INA required that aliens show a "well-founded fear" of persecution in order to be considered refugees for purposes of asylum. (62) The government required the same standard of proof in asylum cases as in withholding of deportation cases. (63) However, both the Ninth and Seventh Circuits disagreed with the standard advocated by the government and claimed that the language indicated a more generous standard. (64) The Supreme Court agreed with these courts in *Immigration and Naturalization Service v. Cardoza-Fonseca*, holding that the "well-founded fear" language established a different and less stringent requirement than the "clear probability" approach. (65) The Court felt that an alien's fear could be "well-founded" even where the risk of persecution was less than fifty percent. (66) Thus, different standards of proof are mandated for asylum and withholding of deportation applications. (67)

B. REMAINING UNCERTAINTIES

Despite the *Stevic* and *Cardoza-Fonseca* decisions, there remained ambiguous language in the Refugee Act to which the circuit courts gave varying interpretations. (68) The terms that have led to a disparity among the circuits are "well-founded fear" and "refugee." In addition, there was continuing disagreement among the circuits as to the proper standard of review for BIA decisions.

1. *Well-Founded Fear.*—Although the Supreme Court decided in *Cardoza-Fonseca* that "well-founded fear"

meant something less than "clear probability," it refused to define the term any further, (69) other than to note that it included both subjective and objective components. (70) In turn, some of the circuit courts have adopted contradictory definitions of "well-founded fear." (71) The Ninth and Seventh Circuits have differing standards for the extent to which a subjective fear must be supported by objective facts. (72) The Fifth Circuit has emphasized the objective component, finding that a "well-founded fear" exists if "a reasonable person in the applicant's circumstances would fear persecution. (73) Similarly, the BIA has adopted this "reasonable person" definition of "well-founded fear." (74) The Second, (75) Third, (76) Fourth (77) and Seventh (78) Circuits are in accord with the BIA's and Fifth Circuit's approach. Perhaps the strictest requirement for showing a "well-founded" fear is that of the Sixth and Tenth Circuits, which have required aliens to show that they possessed "good reason to fear persecution" on one of several specified grounds. (79) Thus, as one commentator has summarized, "there remains considerable room for dispute over just how much more of a showing" is required to prove a "well-founded fear." (80)

   2. Definition of "Refugee."—The "refugee" definition in section 101 of the Refugee Act contains several undefined terms, which the Court had never explored until the *Elias-Zacarias* decision. Specifically, the terms "persecution, (81) "social group" and "political opinion" have spawned controversy and confusion. (82) In general, the Ninth Circuit broadly interpreted the language to make it easier for aliens to obtain refugee status, while the INS strictly interpreted the language.

Addressing the political situations in a number of countries, one commentator recognized "the difficulties of proving individualized persecution in countries where political oppression is non-specific. (83) For that very reason, the Ninth Circuit has found that in some circumstances political neutrality may constitute "political opinion" for purposes of political asylum and deportation. (84) The Ninth Circuit also recognized that a persecutor could easily interpret a person's neutrality as an expression of political opposition and hostility. (85) The First, (86) Fourth, (87) Fifth, (88) and Seventh (89) Circuits have taken note of, but have not adopted, the Ninth Circuit's finding. (90) The government, however, rejected the Ninth Circuit's finding, requiring instead some overt political activity on the part of the applicant. (91) Neither the courts of appeals nor the INS clearly distinguished between aliens who had been overtly neutral (e.g., a vocal conscientious objector) and those who had quietly chosen not to take sides.

Additionally, the Ninth Circuit found that "persecution on account of. . . political opinion" can be based on the political motives of the persecutor. (92) That is, a guerrilla group's attempt to conscript citizens would be political persecution if the guerrillas' general purpose was political. The Eleventh Circuit found that proposition dangerously expansive. (93) Similarly, the government recently argued that this interpretation would allow "draft dodgers" to be eligible for asylum. (94)

3. *Standard of Review.*—Finally, the courts of appeals have differed over the standard of review for BIA asylum decisions. (95) The Refugee Act gave the Attorney General discretion to grant asylum to an alien, and the courts unanimously reviewed that decision on an abuse of

discretion basis. (96) However, a majority of courts, namely the Second, (97) Fourth, (98) Fifth, (99) Sixth, (100) Seventh, (101) Eighth, (102) Ninth, (103) Tenth (104) and Eleventh, (105) more closely reviewed the INS's determination of refugee status. These circuits viewed this component of the asylum decision as a question of fact and therefore reversible if not supported by "substantial evidence." For these courts, the substantial evidence standard allowed for close scrutiny of the BIA's decisions. Other circuits, namely the First (106) and Third, (107) viewed "substantial evidence" as requiring a highly deferential asylum standard. The disagreement over the meaning of "substantial evidence" reflected a wider confusion over the differences, if any, between the substantial evidence and abuse of discretion standards of review. (108)

4. Court Patterns.—The most recent prior Supreme Court decision on immigration, *Immigration and Naturalization Service v. Cardoza-Fonseca*, (109) constituted a victory for refugee advocates, establishing a more lenient standard of proof for granting asylum than that forwarded by the government. (110) However, the strong conservative dissent by Justice Powell (111) and the grudgingly composed concurrence by Justice Scalia (112) indicated the possibility that the Court would swing in a different direction in future cases. (113)

IV. ANALYSIS

Elias-Zacarias left untouched the Supreme Court's earlier decisions establishing standards of proof for asylum and withholding of deportation. The Court focused on the definition of "refugee" in the asylum section of the Refugee Act and the ability of the courts of appeals to review the BIA's decision as to whether a particular alien meets that definition.

A. "PERSECUTION ON ACCOUNT OF... POLITICAL OPINION" (114)

The Court decisively rejected the notion that forced conscription constituted "persecution on account of . . . political opinion." (115) The Court gave three reasons for its adamant rejection of this proposition.

First, the Court refused to accept political neutrality as a "political opinion" within the meaning of the statute: "Elias-Zacarias appears to argue that not taking sides with any political faction is itself the affirmative expression of a political opinion. That seems to us not ordinarily so ..." (116) Thus, the Court rejected the Ninth Circuit's argument, expressed in *Zacarias* and its preceding decisions, that a conscious decision to remain politically neutral did satisfy the definition of "political opinion." (117) The Court ignored the Ninth Circuit's concern that not recognizing political neutrality would undermine a "basic" purpose of the Refugee Act of 1980 because it would limit protection to ideological extremists." (118)

The Court categorized Elias-Zacarias' position as apolitical and then rejected the notion that aliens could take seemingly political positions for apolitical reasons and still qualify for asylum (119)—an idea supported by the Ninth Circuit and the dissenters in the *Elias- Zacarias* decision. (120) Justice Scalia speculated that Elias-Zacarias' refusal to join the guerrillas could have many non-political bases, including "fear of combat, a desire to remain with one's family and friends, [and] a desire to earn a better living in civilian life ...." (121) According to the Court, the actions for which applicants claim they will be persecuted must have had a clear political motivation; that is, the aliens must have consciously attempted to make a political statement through their words or actions. In the future, this argument may be used to exclude aliens who, while lacking an actual political opinion, are mistakenly perceived as holding one. (122)

Second, the Court determined that the "political opinion" must belong to the alien rather than the persecutor. (123) The Court found that "[t]he ordinary meaning of the phrase 'persecution on account of... political opinion' in § 101 (a) (42) is persecution on account of the victim's political opinion, not the persecutor's." (124) The politics of the persecutor are not relevant. (125) The majority thereby rejected the Ninth Circuit's view that the politics of both victim and persecutor should be examined as part of the asylum decision. The Ninth Circuit, in an earlier decision, had refused to give the federal statute such a "restrictive or mechanical ... construction," stating:

> "Persecution" occurs only when there is a difference between the persecutor's views or status and that of the victim; it is oppression which is inflicted on groups or individuals because of a difference that the persecutor will not tolerate. For this reason, in determining whether threats or violence constitute political persecution, it is permissible to examine the motivation of the persecutor; we may look at the political views and actions of the entity or individual responsible for the threats or violence, as well as to the victim's, and we may examine the relationship between the two. (126)

The Supreme Court, however, did not hesitate to adopt this "restrictive or mechanical . . . construction." In so doing, the Court eliminated from consideration for refugee status those who lack overt political positions themselves, but who are adversely affected by groups with clear political agendas. (127)

Finally, the Court indicated that the persecution must stem from the persecutor's displeasure with the victim's political opinion. (128) The Court found that Elias-Zacarias failed this test because the guerrillas were motivated by a desire to increase their army and not because they disliked Elias-Zacarias' neutral position. (129) In *Arteaga v. Immigration and Naturalization Service*, the Ninth Circuit had rejected the need to examine whether the persecutor's motives towards the victim were specifically targeted at the victim's political views. (130) In that decision, the Ninth Circuit required only that the general motive of the persecutor be political in nature.

> It is not relevant that the guerrillas may have been interested in conscripting Arteaga to fill their ranks rather than to "punish" Arteaga's neutrality. To find political persecution, all we need inquire of the guerrillas' motive is whether that motive is political. Clearly, forced recruitment into the war against the government is politically motivated. (131)

The Court's holding in *Elias-Zacarias* significantly narrowed the definition of refugee. But it is important to note that the withholding of deportation section also uses the phrase "persecution on account of . . . political opinion."' (132) In the future, the Court's decision will undoubtedly be extended to withholding of deportation applications. The effect will be that obtaining asylum *and* withholding of deportation will be significantly more difficult for aliens than in the past.

B. STANDARD OF REVIEW

The Supreme Court rejected the proposition, which was held by a majority of the courts of appeals, that refugee status is a factual determination subject to a substantial evidence standard of review. Rather, it established an even more deferential standard of review for asylum and deportation cases. (133) This will significantly restrict the ability of the circuit courts to reverse BIA rulings. (134)

Before *Elias-Zacarias*, many circuits recognized that the Refugee Act of 1980 gave the Attorney General great discretion in granting asylum. (135) However, several circuits held that the threshold step to that decision—determination of whether an applicant met the definition of "refugee"—was a question of fact. (136) Under traditional rules, the test was that an administrative agency's findings of fact could be reversed if it was not supported by substantial evidence. (137) The Ninth Circuit had previously applied this standard to a number of other situations involving decisions by the BIA and other administrative agencies. (138) But some Ninth Circuit judges had also recognized that circuits sometimes used an abuse of discretion standard, thereby giving greater deference to the BIA rulings. (139) On a policy level, some commentators decried the pattern of courts of appeals reversals of BIA decisions as improper interference that prevented the establishment of a uniform national asylum policy. (140)

The Supreme Court had not resolved this disparity among the circuits. However, in his dissent in *Cardoza-Fonseca*, Justice Powell espoused the more conservative view that the BIA, as an administrative agency, should be granted wide latitude. (141) Justice Powell implied that the only grounds on which he would have overturned the BIA's interpretation of the statute would have been if that interpretation was "unreasonable." (142) Referring to the BIA as an "expert agency," he argued that the standard of review issue for both asylum and withholding of deportation was "a question best answered by an entity familiar with the types of evidence and issues that arise in such cases." (143) In his *Cardoza-Fonseca* concurrence, Justice Scalia also expressed his concern that the majority had tolerated less deference to the BIA than was warranted. (144)

Justice Scalia finally secured a majority for his deferential position in *Elias-Zacarias*. Without great explanation, the Court rejected the Ninth Circuit's approach and applied an abuse of discretion standard to both the refugee determination and the decision whether to grant asylum. (145) The Court quoted the portion of the INA indicating that a court of appeals must affirm the agency's "findings of fact, if supported by reasonable, substantial, and probative evidence on the record considered as a whole ...." (146) Justice Scalia interpreted this language to mean that a court of appeals could reverse the BIA only if the evidence existed so strongly in the alien's favor that it compelled any reasonable fact-finder to find in favor of the alien. (147) The Court did not explain why it read this language in this particular way. If one places emphasis on the word "reasonable," then the standard is similar to that of abuse of discretion. However, if one places emphasis on the word "substantial," the standard is closer to the Ninth Circuit's more generous substantial evidence test. Justice Scalia clearly took the former view. (148)

The Court's decision will greatly limit the ability of the courts of appeals to review BIA decisions for consistency, fairness, and appropriateness. Only glaringly unreasonable decisions will be overturned. (149) Thus, BIA decisions, and the ideological biases upon which they may be based, will go largely unchecked by the judiciary. (150)

In addition, and perhaps more importantly, the Court's construction of the term "substantial evidence" will likely affect the judicial review of agency decisions in areas other than immigration law. Notably, the broadly applicable Administrative Procedures Act uses the same key language. (151)

C. STATUTORY CONSTRUCTION

Before *Elias-Zacarias*, the Supreme Court adhered to "the longstanding principle of construing any lingering ambiguities in deportation statutes in favor of the alien." (152) This policy was based on the Court's sense of the seriousness of deporting someone into a potentially dangerous position. (153) After *Elias-Zacarias,* this tendency is seen in the views of only a minority of the Justices. (154) In *Elias-Zacarias*, the Court interpreted the statutory terms "political opinion" and "persecution" in a way that substantially and adversely affects an alien with a questionable claim.

In making its decision, the *Elias-Zacarias* Court focused almost exclusively on the words of the statute itself, with little acknowledgement of the intent and history behind the language. An "ordinary meaning" approach had surfaced periodically in the Court's previous statutory construction decisions. (155) This interpretive technique, however, earned only limited recognition with regard to immigration law prior to *Elias-Zacarias*. (156) Yet, Justice Scalia's *Cardoza-Fonseca* concurrence provided a preview of its emerging form.

Rejecting the majority's willingness to consider "'clearly expressed legislative intention' contrary to [the statutory] language," (157) Justice Scalia in *Cardoza-Fonseca* asserted that the Court should never go beyond the clear, "plain meaning" of statutory language in the "absence of patent absurdity." (158) Where the words themselves are unambiguous, examination of the legislative history is "gratuitous" and inappropriate. (159)

In *Elias-Zacarias*, the Court adopted and reaffirmed this method of statutory construction, (160) despite apparent ambiguities in the pivotal terms. Justice Scalia focused purely on the text of the INA statute and its plain meaning. He held, "The ordinary meaning of the phrase 'persecution on account of ... political opinion' in [section] 101 (a) (42) is persecution on account of the victim's political opinion, not the persecutor's." (161) In so finding, he made an important statutory distinction where none existed previously by rejecting the Ninth Circuit's interpretation of the crucial statutory language. (162) Further, Justice Scalia quite possibly may have circumvented the congressional intent behind the Refugee Act of 1980 to prevent ideologically slanted and arbitrary decisions. (163)

CONCLUSION

The *Elias-Zacarias* decision will make avoidance of deportation and qualification for political asylum more difficult for aliens who fear political persecution. They will be required, at their first administrative hearing, to show that they have a "well-founded fear" of persecution which is the direct result of an actual, explicit and conscious political statement on their part. In addition, the courts will have diminished authority to oversee decisions of the BIA. The standard of review is now virtually solidified as abuse of discretion for the entire decision, including the determination of whether an alien meets the definition of "refugee." No longer will immigration statutes be applied to favor aliens. The reach of *Elias-Zacarias* will extend beyond immigration disputes. The Court's decision decreases the ability of federal courts to look behind statutory language to reveal deeper meanings and legislative intent. Justice Scalia's fixation on the "plain meaning" of the actual words themselves has won a majority position.

1. Do you find this ruling to be troubling? Why should the burden of proof fall on a refugee to show his or her persecutor acted politically?

TRANSCRIPT OF "IN MIXED RULING, SUPREME COURT OVERTURNS PARTS OF ARIZONA'S S.B. 1070, UPHOLDS 'SHOW ME YOUR PAPERS,'" FROM *DEMOCRACY NOW!*, JUNE 26, 2012

NERMEEN SHAIKH: On Monday, the Supreme Court issued its long-awaited ruling on Arizona's anti-immigrant law known as S.B. 1070. The court struck down three of the law's four provisions that subject undocumented immigrants to criminal penalties for seeking work or failing to carry immigration papers at all times. In each case, the majority said those powers rest with the federal government, not with Arizona. But in a unanimous decision, the justices upheld the law's controversial Section 2B, which requires police to check the immigration status of people they stop before releasing them. Arizona's Republican Governor Jan Brewer hailed the decision to uphold what she called the "heart of the law."

> GOV. JAN BREWER: So today is a day when the key components of our efforts to protect the citizens of Arizona, to take up the fight against illegal immigration in a balanced and constitutional way has unanimously been vindicated by the highest court in the land.

NERMEEN SHAIKH: Arizona Governor Jan Brewer. Critics of the controversial "show me your papers" provision say it puts people of color at risk of racial profiling. The Justice Department has already sued Maricopa County Sheriff Joe Arpaio for engaging in a, quote, "pattern or practice of unlawful discrimination" aimed at Latinos. Meanwhile, Arpaio said Monday's ruling would have little impact on how his officers operate.

> SHERIFF JOE ARPAIO: I think this is a good section that has been upheld. I would have liked to see where we would have the authority to arrest illegal aliens just by being here illegally and book them into our jails, but that's not going to happen. But I think this sends a message that we will be involved in enforcing the illegal alien laws and our police officers will be able to at least try to determine if they're in this country illegally.

AMY GOODMAN: After the Supreme Court's ruling, the Justice Department set up a hotline to report potential civil rights concerns related to S.B. 1070. Federal immigration officials followed by suspending joint agreements in Arizona, known as 287(g), that deputize state and local police to detain immigrants. The move prompted calls to end the Secure Communities program, which uses arrest records to target so-called criminal aliens but largely deports immigrants accused of minor offenses.

Well, for more on reaction to the S.B. 1070 decision, we're joined by two guests. In Washington, D.C., Marielena Hincapié is executive director of the National Immigration Law Center. Her group is moving forward with its own civil rights challenge to S.B. 1070 and similar laws in five other states. The suit is filed jointly with MALDEF and the ACLU, which announced on Monday it has an almost $9 million war chest to battle any copycat legislation.

And in Phoenix, Viridiana Hernandez is an undocumented immigrant who has lived in Arizona since she was one year old. She recently turned 21. Hernandez was arrested in March protesting police collaboration with immigration authorities. She now canvases neighborhoods to get out the vote, even though she herself cannot cast a ballot. She's a student at Grand Canyon University. She would benefit from the Obama administration's recent order allowing undocumented youth to apply for a two-year stay from deportation.

We welcome you both to *Democracy Now!* Marielena Hincapié, let us begin with you. The significance of the Supreme Court ruling?

MARIELENA HINCAPIÉ: Thank you, Amy, and thank you for the invitation.

So, as you mentioned at the top of the hour, the Supreme Court's decision has struck down three out of the four provisions of S.B. 1070 and sends a very strong message not just to Arizona, but to other states that are considering similar laws. However, we believe that the fact that the Supreme Court has upheld Section 2B, the racial profiling provision, really has put the Supreme Court on the wrong side of justice. We know from Alabama, which is the only other state where we've seen a similar provision actually go into effect since last September, when the district court did not block that provision from going into effect—we've seen the harm that this has caused. We've seen the racial profiling and discrimination that affects not just undocumented immigrants, but all people of color.

NERMEEN SHAIKH: Marielena, how do you explain the fact that on 2B, in fact, the judges' decision was unanimous?

MARIELENA HINCAPIÉ: Well, unfortunately, you know, I think there's some—the fact that the majority of the court reached that decision, and also when you look at the decision and see that they really struggled with what to do, whether to strike it down completely, they basically have also said that while they think that at this time they don't have sufficient evidence—and remember, the only issue before the Supreme Court was the issue of whether it was preempted. You might remember from the oral arguments, Chief Justice Roberts actually framed the discussion and asked the solicitor general from the United States, ensuring that the argument was not going to touch upon racial and ethnic discrimination. So, in the decision, they have—

AMY GOODMAN: Explain what you mean by "preempted."

MARIELENA HINCAPIÉ: The main argument that the Department of Justice had before the Supreme Court was arguing that only the federal government, under the Constitution and under the Supremacy Clause, has the authority to regulate and to create immigration law. And that's for a whole host of reasons, because otherwise we would have 50 states with different immigration laws. For foreign policy reasons, it's important for the United States, as a sovereign nation, to regulate who comes in and who needs to leave the country. And that was the only issue before the Supreme Court. And in the decision yesterday, the Supreme Court does note that it may—Section 2B may be found unconstitutional on other grounds. And in our case, the Friendly House case, which is the civil rights lawsuit and the class action lawsuit pending, which we are co-leading, we have a number of other constitutional claims, and that's why we do believe that eventually Section 2B will be struck down.

NERMEEN SHAIKH: Could you explain, Marielena, in a little bit more detail the class action lawsuit that your organization is involved in?

MARIELENA HINCAPIÉ: Sure. So we filed our class action lawsuit—it was actually the first lawsuit against S.B. 1070—back in July of 2010, and that was before the Department of Justice filed their lawsuit, as well. And in our case, we are basically arguing that all of S.B. 1070 is unconstitutional and that it should be struck down because it violates the First Amendment right in terms of individuals' ability to assemble—for example, day labor provisions that would impact that—the Fourth Amendment rights in terms of when law enforcement gets to stop and in terms of searches and seizures. We believe that it also violates the Fifth Amendment, due process violations, and the 14th Amendment with respect to equal protection. And that really, at the end of the day, is at the crux of Section 2B, which is that law enforcement officials across the country—and, in fact, even Secretary Napolitano herself, back in July of 2010—said that this provision cannot be enforced without racial profiling. It cannot be done in a racially neutral way.

NERMEEN SHAIKH: Marielena, you've said that one of the effects of the decision taken by the Supreme Court is that it's likely to increase voter turnout by Latinos in the upcoming presidential election. The Supreme Court's decision on S.B. 1070 touches on a number of key issues for many voters. On Monday, SEIU's International Secretary General Eliseo Medina said many Latinos in November would vote against lawmakers who support restrictive immigration laws.

> ELISEO MEDINA: We will in fact say this law is wrong, it will be overturned by the power of our votes, and we will make sure that we have an immigrant system that will do justice to a country of immigrants.

NERMEEN SHAIKH: Obama said Monday he would use the court's decision to push for congressional action on a broader overhaul of immigration laws. Meanwhile, Republican presidential candidate Mitt Romney said the Supreme Court, quote, "should have given more latitude to states on immigration." Can you say a little about the effect of these decisions on the elections, Marielena?

MARIELENA HINCAPIÉ: Well, I think the decision from the Supreme Court, as I mentioned earlier, sends a strong message to the states about what is constitutional and what is not; however, by upholding Section 2B, I think that we in the immigrant community need to see this as a personal call to action. And, in fact, I would say that every person in this country that cares about our Constitution and our fundamental values and that sees that we need to take our country back onto a path that's based on policies of equality and hope really need to get the vote out. And we need to take this to the ballot and vote people out who support laws like S.B. 1070 and racial profiling.

AMY GOODMAN: Viridiana Hernandez is also with us, in Phoenix. Viridiana, first, your reaction to the ruling, and then I want to talk about your own situation.

VIRIDIANA HERNANDEZ: Thank you. Well, as an undocumented student, when I first heard the—what happened in the ruling, you know, it was just a shock, because it's what it is, like something just happened, and although a lot of things, you know, make it, in a way, legal, like it doesn't make it right. And we've seen it throughout our history, so many things that have been legal, such as segregation, it doesn't make things right. And I know that that's something that our community feels and that me, as an undocumented student, knows that this is a wrong thing that just happened to our community, but it just gives us fuel to continue and fight even harder.

AMY GOODMAN: You have been an undocumented immigrant, or, as the DREAMers movement calls it, "undocumented American," since you were one year old in Arizona. You just turned 21. You've taken great risks. You could be deported, but you were arrested in March protesting police collaboration with immigration authorities. Can you talk about your own case, why you're taking these risks? Now, with President Obama's announcement, the executive order, you could become—your situation could allow you to stay in the United States.

VIRIDIANA HERNANDEZ: The risk that I took that day to get arrested, I mean, it's a risk that we take every day. Like, I could be arrested going from school to my house, from the grocery store to my house. So these are not new risks we're taking. These are risks that are now more visible and are challenging, are challenging the system that has been set up in Arizona and just throughout the United States. And so, it's a risk that we take every day already, and so it's like our duty to make sure that people are aware of, like, all the things that happen behind the scenes, because once we challenge them, they're just a lot harder to happen.

And what Obama said, there's been a lot of things said throughout the last few years, and it's up to us to make sure that that actually becomes a reality. But even then, like, the fact that I can leave my house and tell my mom, "Mom, I'll be back tonight," does not change the fact that she can leave the house and not tell me the same thing. And that's why we continue fighting, because our families are still at risk, and our communities are still at risk. And so, there hasn't been no win unless our whole community wins.

AMY GOODMAN: There is one man who has affected your and many immigrants' lives in Arizona more than any other, and he is Maricopa County Sheriff Joe Arpaio. After the Supreme Court upheld the provision of Arizona's law requiring police to check the immigration status of anyone they stop, he was asked how he'd ensure his officers respect people's civil rights. This was his response.

SHERIFF JOE ARPAIO: We do not racial profile. I think we have the most trained law enforcement office in the country, because ICE has trained 100 of my deputies—of course, they took that authority away—plus a hundred of my officers have been trained, five-week courses, federal-trained. So we are well trained to perform our duties in this manner.

AMY GOODMAN: That was Sheriff Arpaio. Viridiana Hernandez, your response? He was speaking on local television in Arizona.

VIRIDIANA HERNANDEZ: Definitely not. As someone that was in the jail system, like I was able to see exactly how they do treat people, how it is that they—that they torment people, that they laugh at people, and those are the things that are seen that a lot of people have gone through worse experiences than me. Like, even in jail, I was still privileged, because the cameras were on, and they still treated me a little bit better than they would have treated other—like they would treat my mom. And so, like, you know, I go door knocking. I go door knocking and talking to people. And regardless of what he says, the people have seen that he is not doing his job, that he is not protecting our communities, that when a community fears the people who are supposed to protect them, there is something wrong. And like the community that we talk to and the community just throughout Arizona see what is wrong with his office, and they're ready to get him out.

NERMEEN SHAIKH: In a rare move, Supreme Court Justice Antonin Scalia's dissent in this S.B. 1070 case also criticized a policy that was not before the court: President Obama's recent announcement that his administration would not deport many undocumented immigrants who came to the U.S. as children. Scalia wrote, quote, "The president said at a news conference that the new program is 'the right thing to do' in light of Congress's failure to pass the administration's proposed revision of the Immigration Act. Perhaps it is, though Arizona may not think so. But to say, as the Court does, that Arizona contradicts federal law by enforcing applications of the Immigration Act that the president declines to enforce boggles the mind." Marielena Hincapié, could you respond to that statement by Justice Scalia?

MARIELENA HINCAPIÉ: So, unfortunately, Justice Scalia's dissenting opinion highlights how ideology really is what's at play. That issue was not before the Supreme Court. The fact that he felt he needed to speak to that and once again question the Obama administration's authority on immigration, at the same time that the court had just issued a majority opinion talking about the importance of the federal government's authority under the Supremacy Clause of the United States, again, just reminds us of the biases that are at play. And so, it's not surprising that that's coming from Justice Scalia. However, I think the important thing is that both the majority decision actually gives more power to the administration and to those of us that have been pushing the administration, like the DREAMers, that have been taking courageous actions through civil disobedience and other organizing to finally get the administration to actually accept and take ownership that they do have this authority and are finally exercising it.

AMY GOODMAN: We only have about 30 seconds left, but, Marielena, can you talk about what's happening in Alabama and other states very quickly?

MARIELENA HINCAPIÉ: Sure. So our lawsuits in Utah, Indiana, Georgia, South Carolina and Alabama continue. Immediately, of course, we're focused on Arizona, so that we will be vigorously pursuing the challenges there over the next days. In Alabama and Georgia, the 11th Circuit Court of Appeals just yesterday did ask us for some additional briefing, specifically with respect to Georgia, and so that's the most immediate next step. But we at the National Immigration Law Center are committed to fight these laws in court until they're struck down as unconstitutional, as well as also working with state and local advocates and DREAMers to ensure that at the state level in 2013 we have states actually pursuing pro-immigrant policies rather than these misguided and unjust anti-immigrant laws.

AMY GOODMAN: Marielena Hincapié, we want to thank you for being with us, executive director of the National Immigration Law Center.

MARIELENA HINCAPIÉ: Thank you.

1. How much leeway do you think states should have in the enforcement of immigration policy?

2. Should federal law preempt, or take precedence over, S.B. 1070? Or do you think the Arizona law has more to do with the enforcement of existing laws rather than a "rewrite" of US immigration policy?

CHAPTER 4

WHAT ADVOCATES AND ADVOCACY ORGANIZATIONS SAY

Geography shields the United States from adopting a more critical role in the Syrian refugee crisis. Unlike Syria's neighboring states, such as Turkey and Jordan, the Atlantic Ocean assures a long, arduous, and expensive journey for Syrian refugees seeking asylum in the US. Still, some advocacy groups are nonetheless actively lobbying against resettling even modest amounts of refugees.

The conservative Center for Immigration Studies (whose slogan "low immigration, pro immigrant" strains the boundaries of logic) is leading such a charge. Below, the group's executive director, Mark Krikorian, retreads the familiar line that resettling Syrian refugees is a potential security threat. Krikorian argues that refugees pose significant security risks, despite being a small and heavily vetted contingent of mostly women, children, and the elderly. Although readers may find it unconvincing that such risk outweighs humanitarian concerns, Krikorian makes more headway arguing that, dollar for dollar, aid is better spent resettling refugees closer to their home region.

Professor and philosopher Philip Cafaro similarly advocates for lower levels of immigration, but he bases his argument on economic and environmental grounds, a position he acknowledges requires difficult trade-offs. Next, we'll look at a profile of Raul Yzaguirre, the longtime leader of the National Council of La Raza, a leading voice for Latino immigrants. His strategies have brought the group much attention in Washington, DC, but his retirement renders the future of the organization uncertain. Finally, we'll read an open letter to President Obama penned by a coalition of immigrant groups. The letter urges reform, a pathway to citizenship for those in the country, and an end to unwarranted deportations.

"THE SYRIAN REFUGEE CRISIS AND ITS IMPACT ON THE SECURITY OF THE U.S. REFUGEE ADMISSIONS PROGRAM," TESTIMONY BY MARK KRIKORIAN BEFORE THE US HOUSE OF REPRESENTATIVES JUDICIARY COMMITTEE, NOVEMBER 19, 2015

HEARING BEFORE THE U.S. HOUSE OF REPRESENTATIVES JUDICIARY COMMITTEE SUBCOMMITTEE ON IMMIGRATION AND BORDER SECURITY, NOVEMBER 19, 2015, STATEMENT OF MARK KRIKORIAN, EXECUTIVE DIRECTOR, CENTER FOR IMMIGRATION STUDIES

A wise man once said, "The supreme function of statesmanship is to provide against preventable evils." Halting refugee resettlement from the Middle East would be just such an act of statesmanship. The starting point of any policy debate is that the government of the United States has no responsibility to anyone but the citizens of the United States. As individuals delegated by the citizenry to deal with the business of the state, the president and members of Congress must necessarily put the interests of the American people before the interests of foreigners.

This means the United States government has no responsibility to refugees; they have no claim on it and no right to demand anything of it. If, nonetheless, we decide as a matter of policy to devote resources to humanitarian refugee protection (a policy decision which I personally support), then we should base our decision-making on two principles: 1) Such policies must not pose a threat to the American people, and 2) the funds taken from the people through taxes for this purpose must be used to the maximum humanitarian effect. Resettling Syrian refugees in the United States fails on both counts.

1. SECURITY

There are two parts to the security challenge posed by refugee resettlement.

A) SCREENING CANNOT BE DONE ADEQUATELY

During last weekend's debate among the Democratic presidential candidates, Hillary Clinton said that the United States should spend "whatever resources it takes" to properly screen Syrian refugees before they are resettled in the United States. This is a common-sense demand that virtually all Americans would agree with.

Officials have assured us that refugees are "are subject to more intensive security than any other type of traveler to the U.S. to protect against threats to our national security." (1) There is no reason to doubt this. The people in the departments of State and Homeland Security, and at the intelligence agencies they work with, are doing their best to protect our people from harm.

But this misses the point. The problem with trying to screen candidates for resettlement from Syria — or any other failed state, such as Somalia, Libya, Yemen, or Afghanistan — is not a lack of resources or commitment.

The problem is that it cannot be done.

Our vetting process is heavily oriented toward electronic checks of databases with biographical information and photos and fingerprints. But little information of that kind which could potentially disqualify a candidate for resettlement is available to us. DHS Secretary Jeh Johnson said last month that "one of the challenges that we'll have is that we're not going to know a whole lot about the individual refugees that come forward." (2) FBI Director James Comey confirmed this, telling a Senate panel last month, "The only thing we can query is information that we have. So, if we have no information on someone, they've never crossed our radar screen, they've never been a ripple in the pond, there will be no record of them there and so it will be challenging."

"Challenging" indeed. We sometimes imagine such information must be available for everybody abroad as it is here – birth certificates, death records, driver's licenses, school records, credit card charges, and all the other tracks we leave behind us as we navigate life in a modern, information-based society

But such tracks are rare or nonexistent in much of the world even in the best of times. And in chaotic conditions like those of Syria – or Somali or Yemen or Libya or Afghanistan – what little existed of the information trail has gone up in smoke. As FBI Assistant Director Michael Steinbach told another committee of this House, "The concern in Syria is that we don't have systems in places on the ground to collect information to vet. ... You're talking about a country that is a failed state, that does not have any infrastructure, so to speak. So all of the datasets – the police, the intel services – that normally you would go to to seek information doesn't exist."

Our screening of refugees resembles the joke where a drunk searches for his lost keys under the streetlight because that's where the light is. The clearest statement of this came from Matthew Emrich, who's in charge of fraud detection at USCIS, when he told a Senate hearing that "We check everything that we are aware of within US government holdings." Because that's where the light is.

Databases are not the only tool used in such screening. Many candidates for resettlement will present documents purporting to show who they are. Mr. Emrich again: "In most cases, these individuals do have documents from Syria. ... Our officers are trained in fraud detection."

Given the pervasive fraud in all the immigration categories overseen by USCIS, this may seem cold comfort, but ICE's Forensic Document Laboratory really does have unparalleled expertise. But the problem with relying on documents is twofold. First, many non-threatening refugees have fake documents too, and that's no bar in itself to being accepted for resettlement. There's good reason for this – people fleeing one faction or another of Syria's war of all against all may well have to lie about who they are to avoid capture or death. But even if we could identify every fake or altered document, how are we to distinguish the non-threatening document fraudster from the threatening one?

Second, the disintegration of Syria (and Libya, etc.) means that *legitimate* blank passports and other documents are circulating widely. Veteran immigration agent Dan Cadman explains: "This is because many Syrian government offices have been overrun in the chaos of war, leaving their trove of blank documents — passports, national identity cards, driver's licenses, etc. — behind for extremist groups and criminal gangs to take advantage of." (3) ICE's Forensic Document Lab has genuine blanks of almost every country's passports for comparison, but that expertise doesn't help when false identities are inserted into these legitimate documents. Cadman again: "In such circumstances, there is no one that U.S. officers can turn to in order to verify the identity of the person who presents these facially legitimate documents."

The vulnerability of documents has been highlighted in Europe this year. Because of the preference given to Syrians, thousands of non-Syrian illegal aliens headed through Turkey to Europe have discarded their real passports and claimed to be Syrian, often presenting fraudulent documents. And one of the Paris attackers appears to have used just such a phony passport.

A final tool for screening refugees is personal interviews. It's true that experienced adjudicators can often sniff out liars and cheats from personal interaction. This works best as a supplement to other forms of screening, not as a substitute. But since those other forms are necessarily ineffective in conditions like those prevailing in the Middle East, pointing to interviews as a substitute is not encouraging. And let us not forget that the State Department's consular officers interview regular visa applicants, as well; but the presence of perhaps 5 million illegal aliens who were issued visas based on their promises made during interviews that they would go home suggests the limitations of this approach.

Finally, one would imagine that a strict vetting process would result in a relatively high rate of rejections. And yet, Barbara Strack, Chief of the USCIS Refugee Affairs Division, told the Senate hearing last month that more than 90 percent of Syrian candidates for resettlement were being approved. How stringent can the vetting of Syrian refugees really be when almost all of them are accepted?

B) THE SEA WITHIN WHICH TERRORIST FISH SWIM

The broader security problem created by refugee admissions – or by large-scale immigration of any kind from societies with large numbers of terrorists – is that they establish and constantly refresh insular communities that serve as cover and incubators for terrorism. However unwittingly, such neighborhoods, and their mosques and other institutions, fit Mao's observation regarding the peasantry's role in China's war against the Japanese: "The people are like water and the army is like fish."

The Brussels neighborhood of Molenbeek, for instance, seems to have been the haven where the recent atrocities in Paris were planned and organized. Its predominantly North African-origin population is certainly mostly peaceful and unthreatening, but they nonetheless served as the water for the terrorist fish.

This applies in our own country as well. Charles E. Allen, DHS's chief intelligence officer at the time, told this House's Select Committee on Intelligence in 2007, "As previous attacks indicate, overseas extremists do not operate in a vacuum and are often linked with criminal and smuggling networks – usually connected with resident populations [in the U.S.] from their countries of origin."

One example of this phenomenon was the al Qaeda cell in the Yemeni enclave in Lackawanna, N.Y., outside Buffalo, which was broken up in 2002. Five of the six members were U.S.-born but raised in the immigrant neighborhood, which the local paper described this way:

This is a piece of ethnic America where the Arabic-speaking Al-Jazeera television station is beamed in from Qatar through satellite dishes to Yemenite-American homes; where young children answer "Salaam" when the cell phone rings, while older children travel to the Middle East to meet their future husband or wife; where soccer moms don't seem to exist, and where girls don't get to play soccer – or, as some would say, football. (4)

No one of these factors, taken on its own, is especially remarkable in our diverse society. Even taken together, the kind of enclave they describe would be of little consequence if it were inhabited by, say, Amish or Hasidim, because those groups do not serve as "resident populations from their countries of origin" for violent extremist organizations like ISIS or al Qaeda or al Shabaab. But communities made up of refugees and immigrants from the Middle East do serve that purpose, however unwittingly – and cannot do otherwise.

The Somali community in Minneapolis is a prime example. Established through refugee resettlement, and continually expanded and refreshed by more resettlement (nearly 9,000 Somali refugees were admitted last year) as well as follow-on chain migration, it has been the source of dozens of recruits for al Shabaab and ISIS, and dozens more supporters. Just this summer, a Somali graduate of a Minnesota high school died fighting for ISIS in Syria. As the *Washington Times* noted, the refugee resettlement program "is having the unintended consequence of creating an enclave of immigrants with high unemployment that is both stressing the state's safety net and creating a rich pool of potential recruiting targets for Islamist terror groups." (5)

The combination of these two security vulnerabilities – the impossibility of vetting candidates for resettlement, plus the growth of domestic breeding grounds – is a big part of why the FBI has some 900 active investigations into domestic extremists, the vast majority related to ISIS. (6)

These investigations come in the wake of many examples of terrorism-related activities by refugees. (All parts of the immigration system have been exploited by terrorists, not just the refugee program; see, for instance, "How Militant Islamic Terrorists Entered and Remained in the United States, 1993-2001." (7) For instance, two al Qaeda bomb makers were arrested in Kentucky after having been resettled as refugees. Nor are they likely the only ones; ABC News reported in 2013:

> Several dozen suspected terrorist bombmakers, including some believed to have targeted American troops, may have mistakenly been allowed to move to the United States as war refugees, according to FBI agents investigating the remnants of roadside bombs recovered from Iraq and Afghanistan. (8)

Other examples: An Uzbek refugee, who presumably underwent the stringent screening that the administration boasts of, was convicted in Idaho earlier this year on terrorism charges. (9) A number of Bosnian refugees, presumably also screened, were charged this year with sending money and weapons to Islamist groups in Syrian and Iraq. (10)

Some have suggested resettling only Christians and other religious minorities from Syria, because we could be fairly certain they would not be affiliated with ISIS or al Qaeda. And indeed, there currently appears to be a policy of discrimination against Christian refugees; Muslims are overrepresented among the Syrians whom we have resettled, perhaps in part because the UN selects the refugees for us from its camps, and Christian refugees fear going to the camps, lest the Muslim refugees kill them, as happened this spring when Muslim passengers on a smuggling boat in the Mediterranean threw 12 people overboard to their deaths because they were Christians.

There are two problems with this approach. First, how would we know if those claiming to be Christians really are? The church records of baptism and marriage that might be useful in that regard are likely either destroyed or inaccessible, and there's nothing to stop jihadists – or even non-terrorist Muslims – from studying up on enough of the high points of Christianity to pass muster. Many Chinese illegal aliens in the United States have successfully gotten asylum by pretending to be members of China's underground Catholic or Protestant churches. How much more successful would Syrian Muslims be in such a fraud, since they are probably already familiar with many of the outward manifestations of Christian practice, given the relatively large number of Christians living there before the civil war?

The second problem with admitting only religious minorities is that resettlement of refugees of any faith is a highly inefficient means of protecting refugees. That issue of effectiveness is subject of the next section.

2. EFFICACY

In addition to the security threats that refugee resettlement poses, any effort to extend humanitarian assistance to refugees must consider how effective it will be. This question also has two facets.

A) MORE CAN BE HELPED ABROAD

Bringing refugees into our country makes us feel good about ourselves. Newspapers run heart-warming stories of overcoming adversity; churches embrace the objects of their charity; politicians wax nostalgic about their grandparents. But the goal of refugee assistance is not to make us feel good. It is to assist as many people as possible with the resources available. And resettling a relative handful of them here to help us bask in our own righteousness means we are sacrificing the much larger number who could have been helped with the same resources.

The difference in cost is enormous. The Center for Immigration Studies has calculated that it costs 12 times as much to resettle a refugee in the United States as it does to care for the same refugee in the neighboring countries of first asylum, namely Turkey, Jordan, and Lebanon. (11) The five-year cost to American taxpayers of resettling a single Middle Eastern refugee in the United States is conservatively estimated to be more than $64,000, compared with U.N. figures that indicate it costs about $5,300 to provide for that same refugee for five years in his native region.

In other words, each refugee we bring to the United States means that 11 others are not being helped with that money. Faced with 12 drowning people, only a monster would send them a luxurious one-man boat rather than 12 life jackets. And yet, with the best of intentions, that is exactly what we are doing when we choose one lucky winner to resettle here.

Some will object that we can do both – relocate some refugees here and care for others in their native region. But money is not infinite. Every dollar the government spends is borrowed and will have to be paid back by our grandchildren. What's more, the U.N. estimates that there are 60 million refugees and internally displaced people around the world. Clearly, whatever amount we allocate to refugee protection will provide for only a fraction of the people in need.

Given these limitations on resources, I submit that it is wrong — morally wrong — to use those resources to resettle one refugee here when we could help 12 closer to their home.

There is little we can do to minimize the costs of resettling refugees. True, the private contractors the State Department pays to oversee the process are making a good living off of refugee resettlement, but reining them in won't make much difference. Most of the costs come from social services; according to the U.S. Department of Health and Human Services, more than 90 percent of refugees from the Middle East receive food stamps and nearly three-quarters are on Medicaid or some other taxpayer-funded health care.

This dependence on taxpayer handouts should come as no surprise. Refugees arrive destitute and often traumatized. They have little education (those from the Middle East have an average of only 10.5 years of schooling), which means that even if they find work, it will pay little. And because they're poor – almost all have incomes only slightly above the poverty line – they pay little in taxes.

Of course, we don't resettle refugees for economic reasons but for humanitarian ones. And since the goal is humanitarian, a wise steward must use his resources so that they generate the greatest humanitarian return. It's also true that refugees brought here will live better than those even in well-run refugee camps in the region. But the goal of refugee protection is to provide people adequate succor until they can return home, not maximize opportunity for a select few.

B) SUCCESS OF REFUGEE PROTECTION MEANS PEOPLE GO HOME WHEN CONFLICT ENDS

A return home is the final measure of the success of any effort at refugee protection. The civil war in Syria, like a similar civil war in the 1970s and 1980s in neighboring Lebanon, eventually will come to an end. Any scheme of refugee protection should be designed with eventual repatriation in mind. The most successful effort at returning refugees to their homes has been in Afghanistan. The UN reports that since 2002, nearly six million Afghan refugees have returned home from neighboring Pakistan and Iran (though many remain). (12)

While the UN doesn't track the statistic, the likelihood that refugees who've been resettled on the other side of the world will ever move back is small. It's not just that the physical distance is greater, though that is a factor. In addition, the acclimation to developed-world standards of living and norms of behavior and the assimilation of children into a new and radically different society make it vanishingly unlikely that those brought here, as opposed to those given succor in their own region, will ever choose to go home.

3. CONCLUSION

Congress has before it a variety of measures to address the Syrian refugee issue, including a temporary pause, a broader change in the refugee rules, and defunding proposals. As you consider how to proceed, I would urge you to keep in mind these two points:

The only way to reduce the security risk of resettling Syrian refugees (or those from Somalia and other failed states) is to reduce the number we resettle.

The government's obligation to make the most effective use of whatever tax monies we decide to devote to refugee protection compels a shift in emphasis away from resettlement and toward protection in the region.

1. The author claims that resettled immigrant populations are "the sea within which the terrorist fish swim." Do you find this statement problematic? If so, how?

2. Do you agree with the author's contention that "more [refugees] can be helped abroad"? Why or why not? What impediments might exist for resettling refugees in their home region, as opposed to the United States?

"THE PROGRESSIVE CASE FOR REDUCING IMMIGRATION,"BY PHILIP CAFARO, FROM *THE CHRONICLE OF HIGHER EDUCATION*, JANUARY 19, 2015

I'm a philosophy professor specializing in ethics and political philosophy, and like many of my fellow academics, I'm a political progressive. I value economic security for workers and their families, and support a much more equal distribution of wealth, strong and well-enforced environmental-protection laws, and an end to racial discrimination in the United States. I want to maximize the political power of common citizens and limit the influence of large corporations. My political heroes include the three Roosevelts (Teddy, Franklin, and Eleanor), Rachel Carson, and Martin Luther King Jr.

I also want to reduce immigration into the United States. If this combination strikes you as odd, you aren't alone. Friends, political allies—even my mother the social worker—shake their heads (or worse) when I bring up the subject. I've been called a "nativist" and a "racist" (thankfully not by Mom), been picketed on my own campus, and had close academic friendships strained.

I can understand why progressives embrace mass immigration (though that embrace is shared, I can't help pointing out, by the U.S. Chamber of Commerce and the editorial board of the *Wall Street Journal*). This is not an easy issue for us, because vital interests are at stake, and no one set of policies can accommodate all of them.

Consider two stories from among the hundreds I've heard while researching this subject:

It's lunchtime on a sunny October day, and I'm talking with Javier Morales, an electrician's assistant, at a home-construction site in Longmont, Colo., near Denver. Javier studied to be an electrician in Mexico but could not find work after completing school. You have to pay corrupt officials up to two years' wages just to start a job, he explains. "Too much corruption," he says, a refrain I find repeated often by Mexican immigrants.

So, in 1989, Javier came to the United States, undocumented, working various jobs in food preparation and construction. He has lived in Colorado for nine years and has a wife (also here illegally) and two girls, ages 7 and 3. He misses his family back in Mexico, but to his father's entreaties to come home, he replies that he needs to consider his own family now. One of the things Javier likes most about the United States is that we have rules that are fairly enforced, unlike in Mexico, where a poor man lives at the whim of corrupt officials.

Still, he thinks that the presence of too many immigrants lowers wages in construction for everyone— including previous immigrants like him.

Javier's boss, Andy, thinks that immigration levels are too high. He was disappointed, he says, to find out several years ago that Javier was in the country illegally. Still, he likes and respects Javier and worries about his family. Andy is trying to help him get legal residency.

I interviewed Javier a few years ago, at a time when the federal government was increasing immigration enforcement—including a well-publicized raid at a nearby meatpacking plant that caught hundreds of workers in the country illegally—leading to a lot of worry among such immigrants. Javier and his wife used to go to restaurants or stores without a second thought; now they are sometimes afraid to go out. "Sometimes," Javier says, "I dream in my heart, 'If you no want to give me paper for residence, or whatever, just give me permit for work.'"

A few months later I'm back in Longmont, eating a 6:30 breakfast at a cafe out by the interstate with Tom Kenney. Fit and alert, Tom looks to be in his mid-40s. Born and raised in Denver, he has been spraying custom finishes on drywall for 25 years and has had his own company since 1989. At one point, he employed 12 people running three trucks. Now it's just him and his wife. "Things have changed," he says.

Although it has since cooled off, residential and commercial construction was booming when I interviewed Tom. Even so, he says, the main "thing that has changed" is the number of immigrants in construction. When he got into the business, it was almost all native-born workers. Today the informal estimates I hear from contractors of the number of immigrant workers in Northern Colorado range from 50 percent to 70 percent of the total construction work force. Some trades, like pouring concrete and framing, use immigrant labor almost exclusively. Come in with an "all white" crew of framers, another small contractor tells me, and people do a double take.

Tom is an independent contractor, bidding on individual jobs. "Guys are coming in with bids that are impossible," he says. "No way they can be as efficient in time and materials as me." The difference has to be in the cost of labor: Insurance, workmen's compensation, and employment taxes add substantially to the cost of legally employed workers. With the lower wages that immigrants in the country illegally are often willing to take, there's plenty of opportunity for competing contractors to underbid Tom and still make a tidy profit. He no longer goes after the big construction projects, and jobs in custom-built houses are becoming harder to find.

"I've gone in to spray a house, and there's a guy sleeping in the bathtub, with a microwave set up in the kitchen. I'm thinking, 'You moved into this house for two weeks to hang and paint it, you're gonna get cash from somebody, and he's gonna pick you up and drive you to the next one.'"

In that way, some trades in construction are turning into the equivalent of migrant labor in agriculture.

Do immigrants perform jobs Americans don't want to do? No, Tom replies. "My job is undesirable. It's dirty, it's messy, it's dusty. I learned right away that because of that, the opportunity is available to make money in it. That job has served me well," at least until recently. Now he is thinking of leaving the business. He is also struggling to find a way to keep up the mortgage payments on his house.

He does not blame immigrants, though. "If you were born in Mexico, and you had to fight for food or clothing, you would do the same thing," he tells me. "You would come here."

Any immigration policy will have winners and losers. So claims the Harvard University economist George J. Borjas, a leading authority on the economic impacts of immigration.

My interviews with Javier and Tom suggest why Borjas is right. If we enforce our immigration laws, then good people like Javier and his family will have their lives turned upside down. And if we reduce the numbers of legal immigrants—contrary to popular belief, most immigration into the United States is legal immigration, under Congressionally mandated levels, currently 1.1 million annually—then good people in Mexico (and Guatemala, and Vietnam, and the Philippines ...) will have to forgo opportunities to create better lives here.

On the other hand, if we fail to enforce our laws or repeatedly grant amnesty to people who, like Javier, are in the country illegally, then we forfeit the ability to set limits on immigration. And if we increase immigration, then many hard-working men and women, like Tom and his wife and children, will continue to see their economic fortunes decline.

Neither of those options is appealing, particularly when you talk to the people most directly affected by our immigration policies. Still, they appear to be the options we have: Enforce our immigration laws, or don't enforce them; reduce immigration levels, increase them, or hold them about where they are. How should we choose?

Acknowledging trade-offs—economic, environmental, social—is the beginning of wisdom. We should not exaggerate conflicts or imagine them where they don't exist, but neither can we ignore them.

There are a number of other choices that we must confront: Cheaper prices for new houses versus good wages for construction workers. Faster economic growth and growing economic inequality versus slower growth and a more egalitarian society. Increasing ethnic diversity in America versus stabilizing our population. Accommodating more people versus preserving wildlife habitat and productive farmlands. Creating more opportunities for foreigners to work in the United

States versus pressuring foreign elites to share wealth and opportunities with their fellow citizens in their own countries.

The best approaches to immigration policy would make such trade-offs explicit, minimize them where possible, and choose fairly between them when necessary. Which brings me back to the progressive argument for reducing immigration into the United States.

Consider first the economic impact of current immigration policies, starting with some key numbers. Since 1965, Congress has increased immigration levels half a dozen times, raising legal immigration into the United States from 290,000 to approximately 1.1 million people annually. That is more than four times as high as any other country. Crucially, post-1965 immigration has been concentrated among less-skilled, less-educated workers. According to a study by Borjas, from 1980 to 1995, immigration increased the number of college graduates in the American work force by 4 percent while increasing the number of workers without high-school diplomas by 21 percent.

The results have been predictable. In economic sectors with large percentages of immigrant workers, wages have been driven down and benefits have been slashed. Employers have broken unions, often helped by immigrant replacement workers. Long-term unemployment among poorer Americans has greatly increased. Mass immigration is not the sole cause of those trends, but it appears to have played an important role. Borjas contends that during the 1970s and 1980s, each immigration-driven 10-percent increase in the number of workers in a particular field in the United States decreased wages in that field by an average of 3.5 percent. More recently, studying the impact of immigration on African-Americans, Borjas and colleagues found that a 10-percent immigrant-induced increase in the supply of a particular skill group reduced the wages of black workers in that group by 4.0 percent, lowered the employment rate of black men by 3.5 percentage points, and increased the incarceration rate of blacks by almost a percentage point.

Significantly, immigration-driven competition has been strongest among working-class Americans, while wealthier, better-educated citizens have mostly been spared strong downward pressure on their incomes. According to an analysis by the Center for Immigration Studies, immigrants account for 35 percent of workers in building cleaning and maintenance, but only 10 percent in the corporate and financial sectors; 24 percent of workers in construction, but only 8 percent of teachers and college professors; 23 percent among food-preparation workers, but only 7 percent among lawyers. No wonder wealthy Americans and the bipartisan political elite that largely serves their interests typically support high levels of immigration.

Our era of gross economic inequality, stagnating wages, and persistently high unemployment among less-educated workers would seem like a terrible time to expand immigration. Yet the immigration-reform bill passed by a Democratic Senate in 2013 would have nearly doubled legal immigration levels. President Obama's recent executive actions to regularize the status of workers in the country illegally respond to genuine humanitarian concerns. Nevertheless, like previous amnesties, they are likely to encourage more illegal immigration by poor but desperate job seekers.

A few years ago, I suggested that progressives truly concerned about growing inequality and the economic well-being of American workers—including recent immigrants—should consider reducing immigration, at least in the short term. Congress can decrease immigration levels as well as raise them, I said. Perhaps a moratorium on nonessential immigration was in order, until the official unemployment rate declined below 5 percent and stayed there for several years, or until real wages for the bottom half of American workers increased by 25 percent or more. While there is debate about the role of immigration reduction in gains by unions, tightening up labor markets after World War II did coincide with the golden age of the American labor movement, a time of high union membership and strong gains in wages and benefits for American workers. It seems worth a try today, particularly given the paucity of other proposals to address the intractable problem of inequality.

I started thinking about limiting immigration 25 years ago, as a graduate student studying American history at the University of Georgia and a budding environmental activist working to kill a dam project in the Southeast. I still recall my sinking feeling as I read, toward the start of the environmental-impact statement on the Oconee River flood-control project, the 50-year population projections for northeast Georgia. Was it possible that our region's population was going to grow that fast? And, if so, how could we argue effectively against building a new reservoir? (We couldn't. The reservoir got built.)

Since that time, I've worked on many environmental campaigns, typically at the local or state levels. In every instance—sprawl, destructive off-road vehicle use, water pollution, ski-area expansion, you name it—population growth was worsening the problem we sought to remedy. And in every instance, we decided not to talk about population matters—either because we thought it would be too controversial, or because we couldn't identify any accessible levers through which to influence population policies.

If they think about population at all, most Americans see it as a problem for the "developing world." But at 320 million people, the United States is the third-most-populous nation on earth, and given our high per-capita consumption rates and outsize global ecological footprint a good case can be made that we are the world's most overpopulated country right now. Furthermore, our 1 percent annual growth rate—higher than many developing nations—has America on track to double its population by the end of this century.

Whether we look at air pollution or wildlife-habitat losses, excessive water withdrawals from our rivers or greenhouse-gas emissions, Americans are falling far short of creating an ecologically sustainable society—and our large and growing numbers appear to be a big part of the problem. Take sprawl. Defined as new resource-intensive development on the fringes of existing urban areas, sprawl has many causes, including transportation policies that favor building roads over mass transit and zoning laws that encourage "leapfrog" developments far beyond existing developed areas. But according to a thorough study by Roy Beck, Leon Kolankiewicz, and Steven Camarota on the causes of sprawl in the United States, population growth accounts for more than half of the problem. While reducing per-capita land use is important in reducing sprawl, we cannot simply ignore its most powerful driver: ever more "capitas."

A similar logic appears to hold for most of our other major environmental problems. I live in Colorado, and my conservation focus has shifted to the rivers of the arid West. Over the past 40 years, declines in per-capita water use in the western United States have been matched by equivalent increases in population. With the low-hanging conservation "fruit" (fixing leaks in urban areas, lining drainage ditches in rural areas, etc.) already picked and population continuing to increase, pressure is growing to build more dams and siphon more water from already overallocated rivers, including the Cache la Poudre River, running through Fort Collins. I love the Cache, and so do many people here; my town has spent millions of dollars to buy land and preserve parks and other open space along the river. If our population wasn't growing, no one would be proposing a big new reservoir; in fact, there remain opportunities to save water through conservation and put more of it back in the river, where it belongs. But an ever-growing population will take such conservation measures, swallow them with hardly a thank you, and demand more. At some point, that means new dams and reservoirs and a dried-out Cache la Poudre River.

Such examples suggest that we Americans cannot meet our important environmental challenges without stabilizing our population. So I've argued that American environmentalists should support significant reductions in immigration. I expected to be attacked from the right, and I was. More surprising have been the assaults from the left. Thankfully, once we actually begin discussing the issues, civility usually reigns, and considerable common ground can be found. Still, I sometimes find it hard to get past people's resentment toward me for bringing up what is obviously an uncomfortable topic. I guess I can understand that; as the grandson of immigrants, I'm made uncomfortable by the topic of reducing immigration. But having spent the three decades of my adult life watching organized labor's power erode and environmentalists tread water, I'm tired of losing.

The good news is that after more than two centuries of continuous population growth, in recent decades we have freely chosen a path toward population stabilization. From a peak of 3.5 children per woman at the height of the baby boom, in the mid-1950s, fertility rates in the United States have declined to 1.9 today: slightly below "replacement rate" for a nation with modern sanitation and health care. That means that if we reduced immigration rates to the levels that prevailed 40 years ago, America's population would very likely peak and then stabilize by midcentury.

The bad news? Just as Americans have chosen to cut back on childbearing, succeeding Congresses have increased immigration, thus keeping our country on a path of rapid population growth. Consider three alternative immigration scenarios—250,000 immigrants annually (roughly the rate around the middle of the 20th century), 1.25 million (the current rate for legal and other immigrants), and 2.25 million (about the level that would result under the Senate's recent reform bill). At fertility and mortality rates projected by the Census Bureau to 2100, we could see modest population growth (to 379 million people), an increase of more than 200 million Americans (to 524 million), or doubling of our population (to 639 million).

Given Americans' failure to create a sustainable society of 320 million people, creating one with hundreds of millions more inhabitants is even more unlikely. And even if we manage to stumble to the year 2100 with 500 million, 600 million, or 700 million people, our unpromising trajectory with continued mass immigration would be further immense population growth in the following century.

Fortunately, such growth, like the flooded labor markets, is not inevitable. We need to remember that the American people have voluntarily chosen to stabilize our population, through our choices to have fewer children than our parents and grandparents did. We can lock in that achievement by reducing immigration rates. That, in turn, could help revitalize the American environmental movement, which, like organized labor, these days spends most of its time in a defensive crouch, trying to protect past achievements rather than reach new ones. An environmental movement with the demographic wind at its back would be much more likely to secure significant reductions in greenhouse-gas emissions, create new national parks and protected areas, and in general move America toward real sustainability. Similarly, a labor movement working within a context of tight labor markets could organize workers more effectively, and negotiate wages and benefits from a position of strength.

The economic and environmental arguments for reducing immigration in the United States seem clear enough. Why, then, do so many progressives advocate for more immigration? As I've learned during dozens of interviews with progressive leaders, the reasons are complex and reflect both the strengths and weaknesses of contemporary American progressivism.

On the positive side, progressives are compassionate. We care about the well-being of would-be immigrants, many of whom are poor and downtrodden. We do not want to tell good people like Javier Morales that they cannot come to America and make better lives for themselves and their families.

We also value diversity. We appreciate the many contributions that immigrants have made and continue to make to American life, and we value the idea of the United States as an open and evolving society.

On the negative side, though, we progressives share our fellow Americans' lack of discipline and inability to think clearly about limits. The answer to any problem tends to be "more," even when it should be obvious that the pursuit of more is causing the problem or making it worse. We dislike economic inequality, for example, but join our fellow citizens in clamoring for faster economic growth—even though under a status quo in which 90 percent of income gains go to the wealthiest 1 percent, more growth just means more inequality. We want to create an ecologically sustainable society, prevent dangerous climate change, and share the landscape generously with other species—but not if it means curtailing anyone's freedom of movement or economic opportunities, or our own consumption. The result is a kind of flabby generosity, in which generalized feelings of good will take the place of focused and effective political action.

Then there is the R word. Progressives are easily frightened by accusations of racism. Immigration debates within the Sierra Club have shown that such accusations can silence or marginalize members concerned about population growth. In my own experience, I've found that critics avoid the substance of my arguments, dismissing them as a cover for nefarious intentions. (Philosophers have been teaching our students for at least 2,500 years that ad hominem arguments are fallacious—but, you know, they still sometimes work.) Progressives' commendable sensitivity to racial concerns can keep us from thinking through what a just and sustainable immigration policy would actually look like.

We need an honest and truly comprehensive debate about immigration and population matters—one that considers Javier and Tom and their grandchildren, along with the many other species that have a right to continued existence. We need to face limits realistically, consider the trade-offs involved in different policy choices, and ask which ones will best serve the common good over the long term. Current immigration policies are ill suited to create an economically just, ecologically sustainable society. We can do better.

1. How and why does this article advocate for reducing the amount of legal immigrants into the United States? Do you agree? Why or why not?

2. Even if the author's recommendations were put in place, couldn't we expect to see more illegal immigration? Would this fact negate the author's well-intentioned position?

"GIVING A VOICE TO HISPANICS," BY MICHAEL ANFT, FROM *THE CHRONICLE OF PHILANTHROPY,* JANUARY 20, 2005

The young Latino activist was aghast as he watched leaders of the National Council of La Raza argue loudly with each other on a convention podium in Austin, Tex. It was clear that the fledgling organization would soon need a new chief to pull it together. The activist looked at the contentious scene on stage, turned to a friend who had also made the trip to Austin, and said, "Man, I feel sorry for the poor SOB who gets that job."

Thirty years later, that young activist—and "poor SOB"—retired as the organization's president.

Last month, Raul H. Yzaguirre sat at his desk at National Council of La Raza for the last time. He leaves the organization much richer and less internally riven than he had found it. Now the largest organization that advocates for the civil rights of Hispanics in the United States, National Council of La Raza has grown from a tiny collection of small activist groups into a well-established operation with 160 employees and an annual budget of $34-million. In addition to advocacy work, the organization provides an array of services to Hispanics, such as housing aid and Head Start programs. Those who have followed Mr. Yzaguirre's career say he built the organization by including all types of people in it.

"He was successful at coalescing regional and ethnic interests throughout the nation," says Roger Cazares, a former National Council of La Raza board member and the recently retired president of the MAAC Project, a San Diego charity that serves Latinos. "The policy issues and advocacy that National Council of La Raza addresses affect all regions and groups. This couldn't have happened if we were fragmented. I credit Raul for having the insight to bring us all together."

REFUSING TO DICTATE POLICY

While other observers say that Mr. Yzaguirre's success at wooing corporate donors has helped the group attain its stature, he emphasizes its grass-roots strength.

"What's been unique is how we derive our power," says Mr. Yzaguirre, who is 65. "We decided we would be an umbrella for community-based organizations, but that we wouldn't dictate to them." Instead, Mr. Yzaguirre and his staff have provided advocacy for the 310 community organizations that National Council of La Raza counts as members and the five million people they represent—and indirectly for the 43 million Hispanics in the United States.

When Mr. Yzaguirre leaves the organization, Latinos will lose a strong voice on Capitol Hill, say some of Mr. Yzaguirre's proteges and other Hispanic leaders.

"Raul has been as influential an advocate before Congress for working families and children as anyone," says Rep. Xavier Becerra, Democrat of California. "He's been able to develop a rapport and a trust—even with people on the other side of issues—that has allowed him to successfully fight for Hispanics and the working poor."

Mr. Yzaguirre has advocated the protection of rights for migrant workers and other immigrants, increased federal financing for programs that educate poor children, and expanded federal income-tax breaks for low-income workers and immigrants following passage of the 1996 welfare-overhaul law, which pushed many immigrants off of welfare rolls.

Under Mr. Yzaguirre's direction, National Council of La Raza and others also successfully worked several years to encourage the federal government to restore $20-billion in welfare benefits to immigrants who legally reside in the United States—money that was eliminated in the 1996 law. Mr. Becerra and others also credit Mr. Yzaguirre with being a driving force behind the creation of an executive commission on Hispanic education in 1990, extension of the Voting Rights Act in 1992, and the formation of the North American Development Bank which, as part of the North American Free Trade Agreement, is designed to help poor towns along the Mexico-Texas border start businesses.

Last month he received one of the highest accolades in the nonprofit world. He received the John W. Gardner Award for Public Service from Independent Sector, a Washington coalition of grant makers and nonprofit organizations.

RUNNING AWAY FROM HOME

Although Mr. Yzaguirre has become a well-known figure in Washington since taking over the reins at National Council of La Raza in 1974, he grew up in more-humble circumstances.

A native of San Juan, Tex., a small town near Brownsville, on the Mexico-Texas border, Mr. Yzaguirre was raised among families of migrant workers. His mother and father, who ran an icehouse and raised cattle, were the children of Mexican immigrants.

At age 13, he ran away from home and joined the crew of a fishing boat in Corpus Christi, Tex. From a fellow worker, he learned about a doctor, Hector Garcia, who was working to improve the lives and prospects of Hispanics. "The more I heard about the work he was doing, such as taking on some big issues—discrimination, segregation, voting rights—the more excited I became," Mr. Yzaguirre says.

Not long after that, young Raul said goodbye to the fishing boat, returned to home and school, and joined Hector Garcia's group—the American GI Forum—in 1954. While he was in school, he spent weekends and holidays working with the group and getting an education in political organizing in the scrub-desert towns of south Texas.

Despite being considered a radical group by some government officials—"This was the McCarthy era," he says—the American GI Forum concentrated on working within the political system, offering scholarships to promising Latino students and, in 1954, sponsoring the first case tried by Hispanics before the Supreme Court of the United States—*Hernandez v. Texas*, which ended a longstanding practice in Texas of excluding Hispanics from juries.

Mr. Yzaguirre formed the American GI Forum Juniors, an auxiliary to the group.

"We came up with the idea that the Forum should become a family organization, like the American Legion," says Mr. Yzaguirre. "We wanted to recruit another generation of people, so organizing became a top priority. We wanted youths to have both a social club and an organization that encouraged them to develop some civil-rights consciousness."

The organization started petition drives urging local governments to start preschool programs for Latinos that were the equal of those for whites. And at a Texas high school, Mr. Yzaguirre was arguing with a principal and his school board about how winners of school popularity contests, such as Homecoming Queen, were chosen. Routinely, the selection process favored whites, even in majority-Hispanic schools.

He would rather have battled for preschool classes or an end to the practice of segregating students by language, he says. "But I learned from that episode that you go where people are. You might try to organize around lofty ideals, but people want their potholes fixed," he says.

WORKING IN GOVERNMENT

The American GI Forum Juniors continued to grow, reaching its membership apex in the late 1960s, but Mr. Yzaguirre wasn't there to see it. After graduating high school, he joined the Air Force in 1959, serving as a laboratory worker at a base outside Washington, D.C.

Upon his discharge in 1963, Mr. Yzaguirre attended George Washington University with the help of federal scholarship money for veterans and became a program analyst at the federal Office of Economic Opportunity in 1966. Shortly before graduating from college, he started the National Organization for Mexican American Services, a group that fizzled because it couldn't raise enough money.

At the time, small Latino groups were scattered around the country and a dozen or so activists kept moving from organization to organization as one folded and another formed, Mr. Yzaguirre recalls. "Same people, different titles," he says.

Mr. Yzaguirre became a consultant to one of the groups, Southwest Council of La Raza, after he left his federal job in 1969, offering the organization advice on garnering federal dollars, setting up an accounting system, and training board members. In 1972, the Southwest Council of La Raza, previously a California-to-Texas organization, became a nationwide group. It moved its headquarters from Phoenix to Washington.

"There was a recognition that to make a difference, the group had to be in Washington, where the action is," says Mr. Yzaguirre.

But he was moving in the opposite direction. He returned to San Juan, where he hoped to do some organizing work before running for local office. He worked part-time there for the Center for Community Change, an antipoverty group in Washington that helps advocacy groups nationwide. Then came the National Council of La Raza conference in 1974. Two months later, he was asked to take over the group. "I turned them down," Mr. Yzaguirre recalls. "But three friends on their board encouraged me to take it."

SEEKING MONEY

Mr. Yzaguirre inherited a group with big ambitions, but no programs, little organization, and less money.

"I had to get resources, which meant tapping the federal government," he says. He was able to get money through federal antipoverty programs and from the Department of Labor, and then Mr. Yzaguirre and his staff of four drew up a comprehensive plan for the organization.

Within six years, the organization's staff grew to 160, affiliates signed on at a rapid pace, and National Council of La Raza was holding an annual conference.

Then, with the election of Ronald Reagan as president, the bottom fell out.

"The government just wiped us out," Mr. Yzaguirre says. Millions of dollars in federal contracts for job training, research, and for increasing staff at affiliate offices were eliminated as part of Mr. Reagan's sweeping domestic budget cuts. By 1982, the organization's personnel list had dwindled to 16 people. Mr. Yzaguirre was forced to take out a second mortgage on his Maryland home to meet payroll costs.

DIVERSE POOL OF DONORS

The collapse taught Mr. Yzaguirre and the organization several valuable lessons, he says: Don't rely too much on government grants and contracts, grow slowly, and beware of taking ambitious contracts to provide services too quickly. To make up for the money losses, the group began treating its annual conference more like a fund-raising event than merely a social gathering, and decided to focus more on advocacy efforts and to be very careful as it started new programs to provide services.

National Council of La Raza also focused on winning attention from corporations, in part by creating a corporate board of advisers that at one point included Donald H. Rumsfeld, who is now Secretary of Defense.

Today, nearly 40 percent of the organization's budget comes from donations made by 100 companies, including Bank of America, CitiBank, Pepsico, and State Farm.

Another 40 percent comes from foundation grants, with the remaining 20 percent from dues, fees for services, donations from individuals, and return on investments. Because of a lack of wealth among Hispanics, getting the support of businesses and foundations is doubly important, Mr. Yzaguirre says.

"We haven't done all that well with individual donations," he says. "The median net asset of the Hispanic family is $0."

National Council of La Raza's courting of corporate donors has been a source of controversy for some activists, who wonder whether business money may cause advocacy groups to moderate their voices. But those who work with Mr. Yzaguirre say he is adamant about not providing protective cover for corporations who might seek it.

"He has been willing to say 'no' to corporations that have tried to buy the organization's silence," says Cecilia Munoz, vice president for research, advocacy, and legislation at National Council of La Raza.

Mr. Yzaguirre says he has never allowed donors to determine where the organization comes down on issues. That policy extends to the federal government, which maintains some contracts with National Council of La Raza—but reduced them after Mr. Yzaguirre criticized Mr. Bush publicly.

"We feel that between $3-million and $4-million has been cut because of a speech I gave two years about President Bush and the promises he has broken to Hispanic-Americans," says Mr. Yzaguirre. "Those kinds of things don't affect what I have to say. No one is going to muscle us."

The White House wouldn't comment, nor would the Department of Health and Human Services, one of the agencies that cut the grants. But the other federal agency that made reductions, the Department of Labor, said the organization was not denied money for political reasons. It was one of several groups that lost out when the agency ended a job-training program, a spokesman said.

ACHIEVING STEADY GROWTH

Since 1986, the National Council of La Raza has grown by about 15 percent each year, even during the recent economic downturn. The organization has reaped as much good will as cash, observers say, because of Mr. Yzaguirre's emphasis on creating leaders.

Several former staff members, including Arturo Vargas, executive director of the National Association of Latino Elected and Appointed Officials, in Los Angeles, have gone on to lead other Hispanic groups, while others have been given a chance to become top managers at National Council of La Raza.

Not long after she first started working for the group, Ms. Munoz says, the National Council of La Raza was asked by the U.S. Senate to testify on what would become an immigration-overhaul bill. Mr. Yzaguirre couldn't make it, so he asked Ms. Munoz to speak in his stead. "I went to him, scared to death, and he told me, 'Just rise to the occasion,'" Ms. Munoz remembers. "I had just started there and to have that vote of confidence from him had a huge effect on me. It also made me aware that the organization was larger than any one person and I had to play my part to make it successful."

Mr. Yzaguirre is also credited by leaders of other organizations with giving them advice and support. Karen Narasaki, president of the National Asian Pacific Legal Consortium, an advocacy group in Washington, says Mr. Yzaguirre went out of his way to help her organization after she joined it in 1994.

"Raul and his staff reached out to me. They said they remembered what it was like to be the new minority community on the block," says Ms. Narasaki, who adds that Mr. Yzaguirre offered advice on how best to build her group and how to increase its influence.

For the past year, Mr. Yzaguirre has provided a more personal kind of guidance. He has been grooming his successor, Janet Murguia, formerly National Council of La Raza's executive director.

Ms. Murguia was previously the executive vice chancellor for university relations at the University of Kansas, in Lawrence, and a former Congressional liaison for President Bill Clinton.

Though he will be stepping down from the top job at La Raza, Mr. Yzaguirre still plans to work to expand opportunities for Hispanics. He is helping to form a handful of programs and centers on community development, leadership, and public policy at three universities in the Southwest, including Arizona State University, in Tempe.

Hispanics have made great strides in the past 30 years, he says, but much is left to be done.

"It bothers me that a third-generation Latino does worse than a recent immigrant in school," he says. "A lack of resources is part of it, but so is a lack of preschool accessibility and lowered teacher expectations. We're making changes, but they're glacial."

1. Have you heard of the National Council of La Raza before reading this article? Do you have any experience dealing with the organization?

2. The article notes that the organization's courting of corporate donors has been a source of controversy among activists. Do you see this as a potential problem?

"NCAPA LETTER TO PRESIDENT OBAMA," FROM THE NATIONAL COUNCIL OF ASIAN PACIFIC AMERICANS (NCAPA), AUGUST 19, 2014

Dear President Obama:

As the Department of Homeland Security (DHS) conducts its review of the agency's deportation policies in order to identify ways to make our immigration system more humane, the undersigned Asian American, Native Hawaiian and Pacific Islander (AA & NHPI) organizations write today to urge you to take swift and broad executive action to address our nation's immigration crisis. Our communities cannot wait any longer. We strongly urge you to expand administrative relief and make significant reforms to the current immigration enforcement system without delay.

The National Council of Asian Pacific Americans (NCAPA), founded in 1996, is a coalition of thirty two national Asian Pacific American organizations from around the country. NCAPA represents the interests of the greater AA & NHPI communities and provides a national voice for AA & NHPI issues. An estimated 1.3 million, or 12%, of the total undocumented immigrant community is of Asian descent, (1) and 74% of voting age AAs are born abroad, the largest proportion of any racial group. (2) Fixing our nation's broken immigration system and doing what we can to address the problem in the face of Congressional inaction is of utmost importance to our community.

There are important changes that your Administration should make immediately to reduce family separation and to protect the rights and dignity of immigrants. Below is a list of priorities advocating specific changes that would have the greatest impact on the AA & NHPI community. Part I of our list addresses affirmative action that the Administration should take to broaden administrative relief, while Part II discusses much needed reforms to immigration enforcement policies.

TAKE AFFIRMATIVE STEPS TO BROADEN ADMINISTRATIVE RELIEF

Under its executive authority, the Administration can allow individuals to remain lawfully in the United States and obtain work permits in cases where an individual has close family or community ties to the United States, as evidenced by the creation of the Deferred Action for Childhood Arrivals (DACA) program. The Administration should use its authority to take the following actions immediately:

Designate Temporary Protected Status (TPS) for the Philippines: In November 2013, the Philippines was ravaged by Typhoon Haiyan (Yolanda), which affected 23 million people and displaced 8 million. The Philippines meets the requirements of TPS and we urge DHS to designate TPS for the Philippines immediately and without further delay.

Create an expanded deferred action program similar to DACA: We recommend granting deferred action with work authorization to (1) individuals who are close family members of United States citizens, Legal Permanent Residents, or DACA recipients, and (2) individuals who have long resided in the United States or have other strong community ties. This type of deferred action relief should also be available to Legal Permanent Residents who may be at risk of deportation.

We also urge the Administration to make any deferred action application affordable for eligible immigrants. Based on experience with the current DACA program, application fees will likely be a significant barrier for many immigrants. The Administration should keep fees as low as possible and make fee waivers and exemptions available. Also, the Administration should consider creating "family applications" with a single fee because many immigrant families will have more than one family member seeking deferred action. Consolidated family applications will also make adjudications more efficient and cost-effective.

Broaden the guidelines for DACA applicants eligible for fee exemption: In order to alleviate the financial burden of first-time and renewing DACA applicants, we recommend broadening the DACA fee exemption guidelines to include low-income families making 200% or less of the U.S. poverty level in the fee exemptions and remove the age requirement currently set at "under 18 years."

Target DACA outreach efforts to the AAPI community: We urge the United States Citizenship and Immigration Services to target outreach to AAPIs by providing in-language public engagements and translated materials in AAPI languages for first-time and renewing DACA applicants.

Expand the current DACA program age limitation beyond 31 and continuous residence cut-off date to June 15, 2009: We support expanding the age limitation beyond 31 years of age and moving the cut-off date of continuous residence to June 15, 2009 instead of the current cut-off date of June 15, 2007. The guidelines should be updated to allow individuals who currently have been in the U.S. continuously for five years and who otherwise qualify for DACA to apply.

Broaden the use of parole for humanitarian purposes: We urge DHS to grant "Parole in Place" with work authorization for anyone with ties to the U.S. and expand the use of "humanitarian parole" to help reunite families with loved ones.

Promote family reunification: We urge the Administration to take action to alleviate the hardship experienced by families caught in the visa backlogs for years and decades. Asian Americans are disproportionately impacted by the family and employment visa backlogs.

One way to end the hardship suffered by these families is by changing how family members are counted for purpose of the visa caps. Current practice counts *both* the principal visa beneficiaries and their derivatives (i.e., spouses and minor children) against the visa caps. This method of counting each family member has the effect of creating even greater demand for the already limited number of visas available each year. However, this practice is not required by statute (*see e.g.*, INA § 203(d)) or regulation. Instead, principals and their derivatives could be counted as a single family unit for purposes of the numerical limitations. For example, using this new counting method, the brother of a U.S. citizen, his wife, and one daughter would be counted a single family unit requiring only one F4 visa, rather than three F4 visas under the current practice. This single administrative change represents a reasonable interpretation of the existing law and would promote family reunification and efficiency. (This change could apply for employment visas as well).

Alternatively, the Administration could use humanitarian parole (*see* INA § 212(d)(5)) to permit family members with pending approved petitions to enter the United States and wait here until their priority dates become current. (The "V" visa included in S. 744 would similarly have allowed certain family members with approved family petitions to live and work in the United States until their green cards became available). We would urge the Administration to issue a policy memo or other guidance making it clear that prolonged family separation is an "urgent humanitarian reason" that warrants the use of humanitarian parole.

II. REFORM CURRENT IMMIGRATION ENFORCEMENT POLICIES

It is estimated that 1.3 million AAPIs living in the United States are undocumented. Between 2009–2012, more than 236,000 AAPIs were returned or removed by DHS. (3) Additionally, over 13,000 individuals have received final orders of deportation to Cambodia, Laos, and Vietnam since 1998. (4) These deportations have separated AAPI families and have sent some immigrants back to countries where they have little or no family connection to the country and sometimes do not even speak the language.

At local, state, and federal levels, racial and religious profiling continues to target minority and immigrant communities through programs such as 287(g) and Secure Communities. Policies that profile have repeatedly proven ineffective, as seen by the National Security Entry-Exit Registration System (NSEERS) (5) and New York City's Police Department's surveillance of Muslim Americans. (6) Additionally, these programs have a detrimental impact on communities, both psychologically and in chilling the First Amendment rights of all Americans. (7) Enforcement measures that rely on racial or religious profiling are ineffective, violate civil rights, and destroy community relationships with law enforcement and other government agencies, thereby making all communities less safe.

The Administration has the authority to reform the current enforcement system immediately to avert the unnecessary separation of families, to prohibit racial and religious profiling, and to create a more humane and effective enforcement system. The Administration should make the following changes:

Expand the use of prosecutorial discretion for people with strong ties to the United States: A presumption of extreme hardship should be available to those with U.S. citizenship or legal permanent resident children and those who arrived in the United States as children or refugees. In the case of individuals with criminal convictions, Immigration and Customs Enforcement (ICE) should bear the burden of proving that negative factors outweigh the individual's positive attributes and the extreme hardship that deportation would cause the individual and his or her family. Alternatively, Deferred Prosecution Agreements (DPAs), normally used in the white collar crime context, could allow ICE to hold removal proceedings of people with criminal convictions in abeyance with the understanding that the respondent would meet certain conditions for a period of time. DPAs are a form of "pre-trial diversion" that could be used to keep individuals with strong attributes or sympathetic facts together with their families.

Prohibit racial and religious profiling in immigration enforcement actions: We urge DHS to eliminate the 287(g) and the Secure Communities programs and dismantle the National Security Exit-Entry Registration System (NSEERS), which are discriminatory and undermine effective enforcement. Additionally, we recommend that the 2003 Department of Justice "Guidance Regarding the Use of Race by Federal Law Enforcement Agencies" be revised to (1) prohibit profiling based on religion and national origin; (2) eliminate loopholes for national security and border integrity; (3) expressly state its applicability to state and local law enforcement who work in partnership with federal government or receive federal funding; (4) prohibit surveillance activities and data collection based on profiling; and, (5) create enforcement and accountability mechanisms.

Provide all forms and information throughout the removal process in a language that the individual understands. All individuals facing removal should be informed of their right to obtain counsel in a language they comprehend. Additionally, they should be provided all documentation and information in a language they understand. An estimated 60% of AAPIs in the United States are foreign born and speak over 30 languages, with a reported 76.5% speaking a second language at home. Many AAPIs are English Language Learners and therefore require in-language information to comprehend the removal process and their rights. Given the broad range of diversity among the group's spoken languages, it is not only imperative to provide culturally and linguistically relevant documents to make the process more comprehensive, this will also prevent unnecessary appeals in the future and lessen the burden on the court system.

Thank you for your consideration of our recommendations. We, the undersigned AA & NHPI organizations are hopeful that your announcement will provide broad relief to the diverse needs of our communities.

Respectfully,

Erin Kessel
Co-Chair
NCAPA Immigration Committee

Erin Oshiro
Co-Chair
NCAPA Immigration Committee

1. Should immigrants from the Philippines receive temporary protected status due to the typhoon? As the number of "climate refugees" increases, could this action set an unsustainable precedent?

2. Which of these reform recommendations do you think stands a good chance of being enacted? Which might be a harder sell?

CHAPTER 5

WHAT THE MEDIA SAY

Among the most disturbing photographs published in 2015 was a picture of a young Syrian boy who drowned when his family attempted to flee their war-torn country. The boy, later identified as three-year-old Aylan Kurdi, was found lying face down on a popular tourist beach in Turkey. Kurdi was but one of countless victims of various human smuggling operations gone awry; in this case, he and his family had been aboard a small boat, headed for the Greek island of Kos, that capsized before reaching the shore.

How does media reporting impact the refugee crisis? Do increasingly common tragic images help refugees find safe passage? Do they elicit sympathy in the West to open doors and borders? Or do these stories merely prove the media axiom "if it bleeds, it leads," and reduce mass suffering to emotionally charged click bait? Unfortunately, the notorious image of Kurdi's body had but a temporary effect. After a brief pause, the human smuggling trade resumed business as usual. Arguably, such media coverage has helped refugees settle in countries such as Germany. However, other nations, like Hungary, have responded with tighter controls at the border. In the first article of this chapter, Rajesh Makwana states that the current refugee crisis demands an ethical response and a global shift from a "culture of war" to one of conflict resolution.

The media are also an important conduit for opposing viewpoints on US immigration. Kurt Eichenwald's article dispels insidious myths that immigrants take jobs from citizens and increase crime rates. In her article "Undocumented but not Illegal," Angelica Rubio points out some of the racist undertones framing the immigration debate, while supplying important historical context in the construction of the so-called "illegal" subject. Finally, PolitiFact's Anthony Cave reports on whether claims that Arizona's economy has improved following the passage of strict immigration laws are true or political embellishments.

"THE GLOBAL REFUGEE CRISIS: HUMANITY'S LAST CALL FOR A CULTURE OF SHARING AND COOPERATION," BY RAJESH MAKWANA, FROM *COMMON DREAMS*, MARCH 15, 2016

THE REAL CRISIS IS NOT THE INFLUX OF REFUGEES TO EUROPE PER SE BUT A TOXIC COMBINATION OF DESTABILISING FOREIGN POLICY AGENDAS, ECONOMIC AUSTERITY AND THE RISE OF RIGHT-WING NATIONALISM, WHICH IS LIKELY TO PUSH THE WORLD FURTHER INTO SOCIAL AND POLITICAL CHAOS IN THE MONTHS AHEAD.

Razor-wire fences, detention centres, xenophobic rhetoric and political disarray; nothing illustrates the tendency of governments to aggressively pursue nationalistic interests more starkly than their inhumane response to refugees fleeing conflict and war. With record numbers of asylum seekers predicted to reach Europe this year and a morally acceptable humanitarian response nowhere in sight, the immediate problem is more apparent than ever: the abject failure of the international community to share the responsibility, burden and resources needed to safeguard the basic rights of asylum seekers in accordance with international law.

Of immediate concern across the European Union, however, is the mounting pressure that policymakers are under from the far-right and anti-immigration groups, whose influence is skewing the public debate on the divisive issue of how governments should deal with refugees and immigrants. With racial intolerance steadily growing among citizens, the traditionally liberal attitude of European states is fast diminishing and governments are increasingly adopting a cynical interpretation of international refugee law that lacks any sense of justice or compassion.

The 1951 Refugee Convention, which was implemented in response to Europe's last major refugee crisis during World War II, states that governments need only safeguard the human rights of asylum seekers when they are inside their territory. In violation of the spirit of this landmark human rights legislation, the response from most European governments has been to prevent rather than facilitate the arrival of refugees in order to minimise their legal responsibility towards them. In order to achieve their aim, the EU has even gone so far as making a flawed and legally questionable deal with President Erdogan to intercept migrant families crossing the Aegean Sea and return them to Turkey against their will.

Instead of providing 'safe and legal routes' to refugees, a growing number of countries on the migration path from Greece to Western Europe are adopting the Donald Trump solution of building walls, militarising boarders and constructing barbed wire barriers to stop people entering their country. Undocumented refugees (a majority of them women and children) who are trying to pass through Europe's no-longer borderless Schengen area are at times subjected to humiliation and violence or are detained in rudimentary camps with minimal access to the essentials they need to survive. Unable to travel to their desired destination, tens of thousands of refugees have been bottlenecked in Greece which has become a warehouse for abandoned souls in a country on the brink of its own humanitarian crisis.

Ostensibly, the extreme reaction of many EU member states to those risking their lives to escape armed conflict is tantamount to officially sanctioned racial discrimination. Unsurprisingly, this unwarranted government response has been welcomed by nationalist parties who are now polling favourably among voters in the UK, France, Germany, the Netherlands, Denmark and Poland. The same is true in Hungary, where the government has even agreed Nazi-era demands to confiscate cash and jewellery from refugees to fund their anti-humanitarian efforts.

There can be little doubt that the European response to refugees has been discriminatory, morally objection-able and politically dangerous. It's also self-defeating since curtailing civil liberties and discarding long-held social values has the potential to destabilise Europe far more than simply providing the assistance guaranteed to refugees under the UN convention. Albeit unwittingly, the reactionary attitude of governments also plays directly into the hands of Islamic State and other jihadi groups whose broader intentions include inciting Islamophobia, provoking instability and conflict within western coun-tries, and recruiting support for terrorism in the Middle East and across Europe.

DISPELLING NATIONALIST MYTHS OF
THE FAR-RIGHT

With the public increasingly divided about how govern-ments should respond to the influx of people escaping violent conflict, it's crucial that the pervasive myths ped-dled by right-wing extremists are exposed for what they are: bigotry, hyperbole and outright lies designed to exac-erbate fear and discord within society.

Forced migration is a global phenomenon and, compared with other continents, Europe is not being subjected to the 'invasion of refugees' widely portrayed in the mainstream media. Of the world's 60 million refu-gees, nine out of ten are not seeking asylum in the EU, and the vast majority remain displaced within their own coun-tries. Most of those that do settle in Europe will return to their country of origin when they are no longer at risk (as happened at the end of the Balkan Wars of the 1990s when 70% of refugees who had fled to Germany returned to Serbia, Bosnia-Herzegovina, Croatia, Kosovo, Albania and Slovenia).

The real emergency is taking place outside of Europe, where there is a desperate need for more assis-tance from the international community. For example, Turkey is now home to over 3 million refugees; Jordan hosts 2.7 million refugees – a staggering 41 percent of its population; and Lebanon has 1.5 million Syrian refugees who make up a third of its population. Unsurprisingly, social and economic systems are under severe strain in these and the other countries that host the majority of global refugees – especially since they are mainly based in developing countries with soaring unemployment rates, inadequate welfare systems and high levels of social unrest. In stark comparison (and with the notable exception of Germany), the 28 relatively prosperous EU member states have collectively pledged to resettle a mere 160,000 of the one million refugees that entered Europe in 2015. Not only does this amount to less than 0.25% of their combined population, governments have only relocated a few hundred have so far.

The spurious claim that there are insufficient resources available to share with those seeking asylum in the EU or that asylum seekers will 'take our homes, our jobs and our welfare services' is little more than a justification for racial discrimination. Aside from the overriding moral and legal obligation for states to provide emergency assistance to anyone fleeing war or persecution, the economic rationale for resettling asylum seekers throughout Europe (and globally) is sound: in countries experiencing declining birth rates and aging populations – as is the case across the EU as a whole – migration levels need to be significantly increased in order to continue financing systems of state welfare.

The facts are incontrovertible: evidence from OECD countries demonstrates that immigrant households contribute $2,800 more to the economy in taxes alone than they receive in public provision. In the UK, non-European immigrants contributed £5 billion ($7.15 billion) in taxes between 2000 and 2011. They are also less likely to receive state benefits than the rest of the population, more likely to start businesses, and less likely to commit serious crimes than natives. Overall, economists at the European Commission calculate that the influx of people from conflict zones will have a positive effect on employment rates and long-term public finances in the most affected countries.

A COMMON AGENDA TO END AUSTERITY

If migrant families contribute significantly to society and many European countries with low birth rates actually need them in greater numbers, why are governments and a growing sector of the population so reluctant to honour international commitments and assist refugees in need? The widely held belief that public resources are too scarce to share with asylum seekers is most likely born of fear and insecurity in an age of economic austerity, when many European citizens are struggling to make ends meet.

Just as the number of people forcibly displaced from developing countries begins to surge, economic conditions in most European countries have made it politically unfeasible to provide incoming refugees with shelter and basic welfare. Voluntary and compulsory austerity measures adopted by governments after spending trillions of dollars bailing out the banks in the aftermath of the 2008 financial crisis have resulted in deep spending cuts to essential public services such as healthcare, education and pensions schemes. The resulting economic crisis has led to rising unemployment, social discontent, growing levels of inequality and public services that are being stretched to breaking point.

The same neoliberal ideology that underpins austerity in Europe is also responsible for creating widespread economic insecurity across the Global South and facilitating an exodus of so-called 'economic migrants', many of who are also making their way to Europe. Economic austerity has been central to the 'development' policies foisted onto low-income countries for decades by the IMF and World Bank in exchange for loans and international aid. They constitute a modern form of economic colonialism that in many cases has decimated essential public services, thwarted poverty reduction programmes and increased the likelihood of social unrest, sectarian violence and civil war. By prioritising international loan repayments over the basic welfare of citizens, these neoliberal policies are directly responsible for creating a steady flow of 'refugees from globalisation' who are in search of basic economic security in an increasingly unequal world.

Instead of pointing the finger of blame at governments for mismanaging the economy, public anger across Europe is being wrongly directed at a far easier target: refugees from foreign lands who have become society's collective scapegoats at a time of grinding austerity. It's high time that people in both 'rich' and 'poor' countries recognise that their hardship stems from a parallel set of neoliberal policies that have prioritised market forces above social needs. By emphasising this mutual cause and promoting solidarity between people and nations, citizens can begin overturning prejudiced attitudes and supporting progressive agendas geared towards safeguarding the common good of all humanity.

FROM A CULTURE OF WAR TO CONFLICT RESOLUTION

It's also clear that any significant change in the substance and direction of economic policy must go hand-in-hand with a dramatic shift away from aggressive foreign policy agendas that are overtly based on securing national interests at all costs – such as appropriating the planet's increasingly scarce natural resources. Indeed, it will remain impossible to address the root causes of the refugee crisis until the UK, US, France and other NATO countries fully accept that their misguided foreign policies are largely responsible for the current predicament.

Not only are many western powers responsible for selling arms to abusive regimes in the Middle East, their wider foreign policy objectives and military ambitions have displaced large swathes of the world's population, particularly as a consequence of the illegal occupation of Iraq, the war in Afghanistan and the ill-conceived invasion of Libya. The connection between the military interventions of recent years, the perpetuation of terrorism and the plight of refugees across the Middle East and North Africa has been succinctly explained by Professor Noam Chomsky:

"the US-UK invasion of Iraq ... dealt a nearly lethal blow to a country that had already been devastated by a massive military attack twenty years earlier followed by virtually genocidal US-UK sanctions. The invasion displaced millions of people, many of whom fled and were absorbed in the neighboring countries, poor countries that are left to deal somehow with the detritus of our crimes. One outgrowth of the invasion is the ISIS/Daesh monstrosity, which is contributing to the horrifying Syrian catastrophe. Again, the neighboring countries have been absorbing the flow of refugees. The second sledgehammer blow destroyed Libya, now a chaos of warring groups, an ISIS base, a

rich source of jihadis and weapons from West Africa to the Middle East, and a funnel for flow of refugees from Africa."

After this series of blundered invasions by the US and NATO forces, which continue to destabilise an entire region, one might think that militarily powerful nations would finally accept the need for a very different foreign policy framework. No longer can governments ignore the imperative to engender trust between nations and replace the prevailing culture of war with one of peace and nonviolent means of conflict resolution. In the immediate future, the priority for states must be to deescalate emerging cold war tensions and diffuse what is essentially a proxy war in the Middle East being played out in Syria. Yet this remains a huge challenge at a time when military intervention is still favoured over compromise and diplomacy, even when common sense and experience tells us that this outdated approach only exacerbates violent conflict and causes further geopolitical instability.

SHARING THE BURDEN, RESPONSIBILITY AND RESOURCES

Given the deplorably inadequate response from most EU governments to the global exodus of refugees thus far, the stage is set for a rapid escalation of the crisis in 2016 and beyond. Some ten million refugees are expected to make their way to Europe in 2016 alone, and this figure is likely to rise substantially with population growth in developing countries over the coming decades. But it's climate change that will bring the real emergency, with far higher migration levels accompanied by floods, droughts and sudden hikes in global food prices.

Although largely overlooked by politicians and the mainstream media, the number of people fleeing conflict is already dwarfed by 'environmental refugees' displaced by severe ecological conditions – whose numbers could rise to 200 million by 2050. It's clear that unless nations collectively pursue a radically different approach to managing forced displacement, international discord and social tensions will continue to mount and millions of additional refugees will be condemned to oversized and inhumane camps on the outer edges of civilisation.

The fundamentals of an effective and morally acceptable response to the crisis are already articulated in the Refugee Convention, which sets out the core responsibilities that states have towards those seeking asylum – even though governments have interpreted the treaty erroneously and failed to implement it effectively. In the short term, it's evident that governments must mobilise the resources needed to provide urgent humanitarian assistance to those escaping war, regardless of where in the world they have been displaced. Like the Marshall Plan that was initiated after the Second World War, a globally coordinated emergency response to the refugee crisis will require a significant redistribution of finance from the world's richest countries to those most in need – which should be provided on the basis of 'enlightened self-interest' if not from a genuine sense of compassion and altruism.

Immediate humanitarian interventions would have to be accompanied by a new and more effective system for administrating the protection of refugees in a way that is commensurate with international refugee law. In simple terms, such a mechanism could be coordinated by a reformed and revitalised UN Refugee Agency (the UNHCR) which would ensure that both the responsibility and resources needed to protect refugees is shared fairly among nations. A mechanism for sharing global responsibility would also mean that states only provide assistance in accordance with their individual capacity and circumstances, which would prevent less developed nations from shouldering the greatest burden of refugees as is currently the case.

Even though the UN's refugee convention has already been agreed by 145 nations, policymakers in the EU seem incapable and unwilling to demonstrate any real leadership in tackling this or indeed any other pressing transnational issue. Not only does the resulting refugee fiasco demonstrate the extent to which self-interest dominates the political status quo across the European Union, it confirms the suspicion that the union as a whole is increasingly devoid of social conscience and in urgent need of reform.

Thankfully, ordinary citizens are leading the way on this critical issue and putting elected representatives to shame by providing urgent support to refugee families in immediate need of help. In their thousands, volunteers stationed along Europe's boarders have been welcoming asylum seekers by providing much needed food, shelter and clothing, and have even provided search and rescue services for those who have risked their lives being trafficked into Europe in rubber dinghies. Nowhere is this spirit of compassion and generosity more apparent than on Lesbos and other Greek islands, where residents have been collectively nominated for the 2016 Nobel Peace Prize for their humanitarian efforts.

The selfless actions of these dedicated volunteers should remind the world that people have a responsibility and a natural inclination to serve one another in times of need – regardless of differences in race, religion and nationality. Instead of building militarised borders and ignoring popular calls for a just and humanitarian response to the refugee crisis, governments should take the lead from these people of goodwill and prioritise the needs of the world's most vulnerable above all other concerns. For European leaders and policymakers in all countries, it's this instinctively humane response to the refugee crisis – which is based firmly on the principle of sharing – that holds the key to addressing the whole spectrum of inter-connected social, economic and environmental challenges in the critical period ahead.

1. The author links Europe's and the United States' "misguided foreign policies" to the current refugee crisis. What do you think about this?

2. Do you think the world has a moral responsibility to help refugees?

"ILLEGAL IMMIGRATION: MYTHS, HALF-TRUTHS AND A HOLE IN TRUMP'S WALL," BY KURT EICHENWALD, FROM *NEWSWEEK*, OCTOBER 23, 2015

Are there any Americans who can't recite by rote the many allegations leveled by politicians against undocumented immigrants? *They are violent, dangerous lawbreakers. They steal jobs from citizens. They cost taxpayers billions for social services. And then there are the proposed solutions: Washington should deport the millions who are in the country illegally and build a wall on the Mexican border to prevent them from returning.*

Lots of people believe all of this, but how much of it is true? And would the proposed solutions be effective, and at what cost?

The answers aren't what most Americans—conservative or liberal—want to hear. Other than their violation of immigration laws, these "illegals" commit far fewer crimes per capita than lesser educated, native-born Americans. They do take jobs, but they also create more jobs for Americans. They use some social services, but a lot of that is offset by how much they pump into the economy. The aggressive enforcement of U.S. immigration laws has given rise to an organized crime network that smuggles people across the border, often while subjecting them to rape, kidnapping and even murder. And as for the most popular, easy-sounding solutions, such as building walls and having mass deportations? They are ridiculous and would require spending hundreds of billions of dollars to accomplish virtually nothing, while upending the American economy.

All of this raises a fundamental question: Is immigration really of such import that finding ways to boot out border-crossers should be a central issue in the current presidential campaigns? Or has immigrant paranoia become the red meat both Democratic and Republican politicians wave in front of crowds, hoping to whip them into a frenzy to win votes?

In other words, we know why the politicians might be lying on this issue. We just need to understand what the falsehoods are.

THE COYOTE MAFIA

To understand the current controversy, look back a few decades. Until the mid-1960s, illegal immigration from Mexico was incomprehensible because the United States was legally admitting about 50,000 Mexicans a year as immigrants. From 1942 through 1964, the United States issued short-term visas for temporary laborers from Mexico, primarily for agricultural work. The system functioned well—some Mexicans became legal residents, more became temporary workers, and very little needed to be spent policing the borders since the laborers were happy to head back home when their seasonal jobs were done.

But civil rights advocates criticized the program as exploitative, and in 1965 Congress terminated the issuance of the short-term visas, which accomplished nothing. "When opportunities for legal entry disappeared after 1965, the massive inflow from Mexico simply re-established itself under undocumented auspices," says Douglas Massey, a professor of sociology and public affairs at Princeton University. "By 1979, it roughly equaled the volume observed in the late 1950s, only now the overwhelming majority of migrants were 'illegal.'"

Fast-forward to 1986. That year, IBM introduced the first laptop computer, *Top Gun* raked in millions at the box office, the Chicago Bears won Super Bowl XX, and the big topic in Washington, D.C., was immigration reform. The number of immigrants coming into the United States illegally had been increasing dramatically since 1979, leading to concerns that they were taking jobs from citizens, soaking up tax dollars through social services and creating innumerable other problems. So the Reagan administration and Congress hammered out a solution. The Immigration Reform and Control Act imposed significant financial penalties on companies that hired these immigrants, provided near-universal amnesty for those already in the United States and beefed up border security. Almost all of the 3.2 million people unlawfully residing in the country applied for amnesty, and about 2.8 million received it. Tougher borders, tougher employment sanctions and no more money or time wasted chasing people who didn't have the necessary immigration papers—it seemed like a perfect solution.

But it wasn't. Farmers railed against the law, fearful that they would no longer have access to the many workers who harvested crops, and the Chamber of Commerce protested the financial sanctions on employers. So, over the years, the requirements compelling employers to thoroughly vet potential hires for their immigration status were rolled back.

Since 1986, the number of immigrants without documentation has exploded, peaking at around 12 million in 2007 and then dropping after the economic collapse the following year. The Department of Homeland Security now estimates that there are in excess of 11 million in the United States. And that may have been the least bad thing that the new laws spawned. The amnesty program, combined with strengthening border security, created a huge demand for bogus documentation so that immigrants who had arrived in the country too late to qualify for the program could pretend they reached America early enough to be declared eligible. Mexicans preparing to head for the United States in hopes of being granted amnesty turned to a black market for counterfeit records run by a network of so-called *coyotajes*—criminals best known for smuggling people across the border. As more money poured into the coyotaje gangs, their power grew. The toughened border patrols created by the 1986 law served only to increase the influence of the coyotajes. Individuals could no longer expect to simply wade across the Rio Grande; instead, they had to turn to the ruthless gangs for help. The increasingly violent coyotaje-organized crime groups became a primary means of reaching America, charging large sums for each person crossing the border. This became a huge enterprise, earning as much as $6 billion a year, says one federal immigration official, who spoke on condition of anonymity.

When organized crime starts making money in a business, business booms. Coyotajes and drug cartels not only helped people who wanted to go across the border but also spent time in their communities convincing others to head to the United States. That's why when politicians now say "let's stop illegal immigration," they may as well be proclaiming that they can end gambling, prostitution, drugs or any other business of organized crime. America is no longer trying to keep out some Mexican men hoping to find work; it is in a war with vicious criminals who can move fast to adapt to any new policies and preserve their billions. They already have: When border patrols were bolstered at San Diego and El Paso, Texas, smugglers began to move toward the Sonoran Desert. This, of course, was more difficult and dangerous, so smugglers increased their fees from $500 a head to $3,000. A large number of border-crossers paid an even higher price— the risk of death for people entering the United States illegally through the Sonoran was 17 times greater in 2009 than it had been in 1998, according to the American Civil Liberties Union and the Heritage Foundation.

Many of those people died either because the smugglers either abandoned or murdered them. Coyotaje groups have even have gone so far as to kidnap people who were making their way to the U.S., then demand payment from the victims' families in exchange for releasing them. And many women who hired the smugglers have reported being sexually assaulted by them.

THE NO-CRIME WAVE

Once immigrants arrive in the U.S. illegally, do they commit crimes? Of course, in any group of millions of people, there will be those who engage in violent felonies, but the numbers here are not statistically significant. Ruben Rumbaut, a professor of sociology at the University of California, Irvine, noted in a 2007 report for the Immigration Policy Center (now part of the American Immigration Council) that even though the number of undocumented immigrants doubled from 1994 to the record level of 12 million in 2007, the violent crime rate in America dropped 34 percent, and the property crime rate fell 26 percent. That same report found that Mexican immigrants—including those who entered the U.S. legally and illegally—had an incarceration rate in 2000 of 0.7 percent, one-eighth the rate of native-born Americans of Mexican descent and lower than that of American-born whites and blacks of similar socioeconomic status and education. And repeated studies have found that areas with high concentrations of workers without documentation—such as El Paso—are among the safest cities in the country. The 2010 census data reveal that young, poorly educated men in the U.S. from Mexico, El Salvador and Guatemala—the bulk of the population of immigrants who live in the country illegally—have incarceration rates significantly lower than those of native-born young men without a high school diploma.

Multiple studies by government and academic groups have found that the vast majority of arrests of immigrants without documentation involve immigration charges, followed by drug violations. For example, a Government Accountability Office report from 2011 stated that 90 percent of all immigrants sentenced for a crime in federal court had been charged with either immigration or drug violations. And included in that mix are the smugglers who were headed back to Mexico but still in the United States illegally for a brief time.

A detailed study by the Center for Violence Prevention and Community Safety at Arizona State University of arrests in Maricopa County—where there is a large population of immigrants—found that those without documentation were far less likely than American citizens to have used marijuana, crack cocaine or methamphetamines, although they were somewhat more likely to use powder cocaine.

The bottom line: The claim made by people such as Donald Trump—the real estate tycoon who is leading in polls for the Republican nomination—that the Mexican government is emptying its jails and sending murderers and rapists into America is ridiculous. The gangs of murderers and rapists—the coyotajes empowered by poorly planned U.S. policy—return home, crossing the border only to keep the money flowing to their illicit businesses. Their clients—and frequent victims—are mostly those desperate to answer the siren song of American farmers and businesses seeking cheap labor.

THEY PAY TAXES!

What about the charge that immigrants steal jobs from Americans? A joint study by the University of Utah and the University of Arizona confirmed that most undocumented immigrants work in low-skilled jobs normally not filled by Americans. More important, though, is this surprising fact: Immigrants create jobs. It's simple economics—if more people spend money, more jobs are created. Workers without documentation still pay rent, buy food and clothes, go to the movies. Just through their daily existence as consumers, they are spurring economic activity. For example, the Bell Policy Center, a Colorado research group, found that for every job held in that state by an immigrant who lived in the country illegally, another 0.8 jobs are created.

And, once again contradicting popular belief, a majority of immigrants without documentation pay taxes. Some use individual taxpayer identification numbers on their official payment forms; others use fake Social Security numbers (the Internal Revenue Service recognizes those are bogus but happily accepts the money). They also pay significant sums into both the Social Security Trust Fund and Medicare, but because few of them qualify for benefits, they take little out. In fact, the Social Security Administration includes over $7 billion in annual contributions from these immigrants in its calculations of the trust fund's solvency.

A series of studies have documented the amounts of state taxes paid by immigrants without documentation. In California, they pay about $300 million a year in income taxes. In Georgia, around $250 million in income, sales and property taxes. In Oregon, as much as $300 million and in Virginia as much as $174 million in tax revenue. In Texas, it's $400 million. And on and on.

THE CURE MIGHT KILL YOU

There are, of course, costs associated with immigrants who enter the country illegally. The tab for law enforcement and incarceration is probably the largest one. A Government Accountability Office report from 2005 found the cost over four years just for locking up these immigrants totaled $5.8 billion, with local jails and state prisons spending $1.7 billion. Today, that number is even higher, as efforts to capture and deport them have intensified.

Then there is health care. Very few immigrants without documentation have health insurance because, contrary to the blather by some conservative commentators, they are not covered by federal health programs or by employer-provided insurance. As a result, repeated studies have found that they tend to delay seeking treatment until a problem grows significant, at which point they turn to emergency rooms. Different analyses conducted by academic researchers have come up with conflicting numbers of the total cost, but the range is from $6 billion to $10 billion a year.

Education is the other big cost. Since the 1982 Supreme Court ruling in the case of *Plyler v. Doe*, public schools have been required to educate children without documentation. A study by Arizona State University and the University of Utah concluded that the amount needed per year to educate these children is $17 billion, which is about 3.3 percent of the total amount spent annually for public schools.

A billion here, a billion there—these are all big numbers. But that is only one side of the equation. The workers also bring significant economic benefit to the country. Take Texas, a state with one of the largest populations of immigrants who crossed the border illegally. A 2006 report by the state comptroller estimated they added $17.7 billion to gross state product, including contributing $424 million more to state revenue than they consumed in government services, such as education, health care and law enforcement. In fact, the comptroller found, if politicians made good on their promises to round up immigrants without documentation and toss them out of the country, Texas would take a punch in the gut. Not only would the state lose that $424 million in revenue, but it also would see a drop of 2.3 percent of the jobs in the state because of the loss of economic activity from those who were removed.

Arizona—the state where some of the loudest calls for tough action on immigration have been made—would also fare badly. The Immigration Policy Center found that the state would lose $11.7 billion in gross state product and over 140,000 jobs if all immigrants without documentation were deported.

Indeed, the nation would suffer significantly if all these people were sent home, according to a 2015 report by the American Action Forum, which describes itself as a center-right policy institute. Such a mass deportation "would cause the labor force to shrink by 6.4 percent, which translates to a loss of 11 million workers," the report says. "As a result, 20 years from now the economy would be nearly 6 percent or $1.6 trillion smaller than it would be if the government did not remove all undocumented immigrants." The impact would be felt across the economy, the report says, although the agriculture, construction, retail and hospitality sectors would be the hardest hit.

WALL-EYED LUNACY

When all the statistics and studies are examined, it is easy to see how deceptive or ignorant politicians have been when discussing illegal immigration. And the real hilarity ensues when they lay out their simplistic proposals of kicking 'em out and building a fence.

Start with mass deportations. Perhaps Americans would be willing to lose that $1.6 trillion when 11 million people are sent back across the border. That, however, is not the total cost here. The government has to apprehend, detain, process and transport those millions of men, women and children. Even with a fence, there will need to be large sums spent to keep the deported from returning. The price tag for this undertaking would be in the range of $420 billion to $620 billion, according to American Action Forum, which also estimates that the purge will take 20 years. That means an immigrant's 5-year-old daughter could be his lawyer at the deportation hearing that will commence decades from now.

And that brings us to the fence. There are many problems with this, the most important of which is that a huge percentage of the 11 million immigrants without documentation in the U.S. didn't cross the border illegally. Some 4 million to 5 million of them simply overstayed their visas. No fence, no matter how high, will solve that problem.

Then there is the issue of the border's topography. Just take the area from El Paso to Brownsville, Texas—which takes up about 1,200 miles of the 1,933-mile U.S.-Mexico border. How would the fence deal with Falcon International Reservoir, which is on the border? The reservoir was created by a dam, which also straddles the border. Would the fence run down the middle of the dam, then drop down to the reservoir and cut through the middle of it, dropping as much as 110 feet to its lowest depth? Or would the United States surrender huge swaths of territory by placing its "border" fence on the shoreline, far from the actual border?

Forget Falcon. What about Big Bend National Park? That runs along 118 miles of border. With canyons, mountains and a river, attempting to build a fence would not only destroy one of the country's most beautiful parks but also be fruitless. The fence would have to go up mountains, to elevations as high as almost 8,000 feet.

These are just a few of the massive challenges presented over less than half of the border. Then there are the broader issues—the billions a fence would cost and the pointlessness of the effort. The Congressional Research Service found in 2007 that a 700-mile fence would cost about $50 billion over 25 years, including construction, maintenance and upkeep. And remember, that number isn't the half of it: The border is 1,933 miles long.

But assume, somehow, that the fence is magically built over rivers and lakes and mountains for a reasonable price tag. Is there anyone dumb enough to believe that Mexican gangsters running the people-smuggling operations will look at a wall, shrug their shoulders and give up a $6 billion yearly business?

Of course not. Instead, boats will start dropping immigrants at Padre Island, just off the Gulf of Mexico but in the United States. Or the smugglers will raise their prices, and ships will take immigrants north, where they can come ashore above San Diego. Or guards will be bribed. Or the fence bombed. Put simply, people who believe violent criminals cannot find their way around a wall are not being honest with themselves or the public.

What, then, should the United States do about illegal immigration? A fence won't work, mass deportation won't work, and every plan the government has adopted in recent decades has done nothing but enriched and empowered crime syndicates that have transformed a modest problem into an intractable one.

Perhaps, then, it is time for the country to take a deep, collective breath, stop trafficking in fantasies and face the reality that the only system that ever proved effective in dealing with Mexican nationals wanting to come to America for work was the one abandoned in 1964, when some were given residence and others received temporary visas. Maybe, in this case, the answer for the future can be found in the past.

1. This article is persuasive, but can you think of any reasons why unrestricted immigration along the Mexican border might be undesirable?

2. What are some political roadblocks that might prevent the author's solutions from becoming reality?

"UNDOCUMENTED, NOT ILLEGAL: BEYOND THE RHETORIC OF IMMIGRATION COVERAGE," BY ANGELICA RUBIO, *FROM NACLA REPORT ON THE AMERICAS,* NOVEMBER/DECEMBER 2011

In June, Pulitzer Prize winner Jose Antonio Vargas came out as an undocumented person. Many advocates were inspired by his story because it put a face on the millions of undocumented immigrants living in the shadows of

U.S. society. Unfortunately rather than participate in the discussion, the mainstream media ignited a firestorm. As *Colorlines*'s Monica Novoa carefully explained the following day, Vargas's story drew "enormous media attention and drove 'undocumented immigrant' up to a top-trending term on Twitter. ... But it's a shame that in the dissection and retelling of his story a fine point has been lost on many of Vargas' colleagues: He came out specifically as an undocumented immigrant and not as 'illegal.'" (1)

The Vargas story is a telling example of the media coverage of the immigration debate in the United States in recent years—inaccurate, incomplete, and insufficient. Vargas himself wrote several months later that after interviewing journalists, politicians, policy experts, and media analysts, there was an "undeniable" consensus that the media framing around illegal immigration was "stuck in a simplistic, us-versus-them, black-or-white, conflict-driven narrative, often featuring the same voices making familiar arguments." (2)

Who are these voices? Where is the overheated rhetoric coming from? Over the last decade, anti-immigrant groups have been on the rise across the country. According to a 2008 report by the Southern Poverty Law Center, the number of hate groups rose from 602 in 2000 to 888 in 2007—a 48% increase. In 2007, the SPLC added the 250,000-member Federation for American Immigration Reform (FAIR) to its "list of hate group" for the organization's baseless anti-immigrant "theories, coupled with a history of ties to white supremacist groups." (3) FAIR is largely funded by wealthy racists, such as John Tanton, who also helped to found the Center for Immigration Studies (CIS), and Numbers USA, creating a veritable anti-immigrant empire in the mid-1990s. According to *The New York Times* these groups were influential in the congressional defeat of the Dream Act in 2010, and the drafting of Arizona's notorious SB 1070 legislation. (4) State legislatures in Alabama and Georgia have followed suit, passing legislation, which, like Arizona's SB 1070, essentially legalizes racial profiling against suspected undocumented immigrants. (5)

Along with the growth of these anti-immigrant groups, and the draconian laws they have helped to pass, is a rise in the anti-immigrant rhetoric. The message from FAIR, CIS, and Numbers USA is one of intolerance, carrying a highly charged racial discourse, which provides ammunition to media conglomerates that capitalize on the negative narrative of immigration, fueling an already fearful citizenry.

In May 2008, Media Matters, a web-based, progressive research center, released *Fear and Loathing in Prime Time*, a report that analyzed the immigration rhetoric heard on cable news. The report focused on commentators who often discussed the issue of illegal immigration on their programs, such as CNN's Lou Dobbs and Fox's Bill O'Reilly and Glenn Beck. The report found that these hosts provided an extremely high amount of misinformation. For example, despite studies that show that immigrants are less likely to commit crimes, O'Reilly and Beck particularly promoted the idea that "illegal aliens" were responsible for a crime wave sweeping the country.

"Number one, the illegal aliens shouldn't be here. And number two, the culture from which they come is a lot more violent than the USA," O'Reilly told viewers in January 2007.

"America's border crisis. Rape, drugs, kidnapping, even murder. It is beginning to look a lot more like a border war," said Beck on November 8, 2007.

Dobbs pushed the popular *reconquista* myth, that immigrants are planning to retake Aztlan—portions of the American Southwest, which the United States took from Mexico in the 1840s. Although these myths are false, they are portrayed as fact on prime-time television, and millions of viewers believe them. They make the term "illegal" scary and violent, and the debate for comprehensive immigration reform much less likely.

"I also know our country is on fire, and the fuel is illegal immigration," Beck told viewers in January 2007. "There are about 12 to 15 million illegals in this country and that number is growing by 500,000 every year. Recent investigations showed that in Los Angeles 95 percent of all warrants for homicide targeted illegal aliens. They put a strain on our Social Security, our education, our health care and, yes, national security."

This rhetoric—particularly the use of the term "illegal"—has become part of the regular media vocabulary. The term dehumanizes undocumented immigrants, depicting them all as criminals.

"Using the word [illegal] ... crosses the line by criminalizing the person, not the action they are purported to have committed," said a September 201.0 press release from the National Association of Hispanic Journalists, a Washington-based organization with 2,300 members. The NAHJ also denounced "the use of the degrading terms 'alien' and 'illegal alien' to describe undocumented immigrants because it casts them as adverse, strange beings, inhuman outsiders who come to the U.S. with questionable motivations."

More recently, the Society of Professional Journalists, a century-old organization with a membership of nearly 10,000, rallied against the term illegal, passing a resolution that "immigrants are undocumented, not illegal." They later presented the resolution to its members at their national convention in September. (6)

The Applied Research Center and its daily news site, Colorlines.com, have even launched the public education campaign, Drop the I-Word. According to the campaign, the I-word opens the door to racial profiling and violence, and prevents truthful, respectful debate on immigration. "No human being is illegal," says their website.

These public declarations are important, despite the fact that mainstream media does not appear to be listening. But how about other, more independent media? In a September article for New America Media, reporter Elena Shore interviewed editors from several "ethnic" media outlets, about the term they use to describe an immigrant who is in the United States illegally. "Before publishing a story on immigration, every editor faces [this] question," wrote Shore. Their conclusions are varied.

Alfredo Carbajal, chief editor of the Dallas Spanish-language daily, *Al Dia*, says that they use the term "undocumented" and have done so since the paper's founding in 2003. However, he says that readers, even among the Hispanic community write in saying that "by not calling illegal immigration 'illegal,' you're already taking a side," Janna Sundeyeva, editor of San Francisco's Russian-language newspaper, *Kstati*, would agree.

"The direct and honest word is 'illegal' because it is actually illegal to cross the border of any country without proper documents," said Sundeyeva. However, Korean media, Shore discovered, often uses the term "over-stayer" and the Punjabi media frequently uses the term "living in hiding," instead of the words "undocumented" or "illegal." (7)

In politics, however, the "I-word" appears to have become the word of choice, especially among Republicans. On October 18, Herman Cain, former Massachusetts governor Mitt Romney and Texas governor Rick Perry participated in the CNN-televised Republican presidential debate in Las Vegas. Aside from duking it out over Romney's alleged "illegal" lawn maintenance worker, Perry and Romney used the term "illegal" 28 times within a 15-minute argument over immigration. It was apparent that not one candidate on that stage was in touch with the plight of the undocumented immigrant. Then again, neither was the audience, Cain's idea of building an electrified fence between the U.S.-Mexico border to prevent illegal immigration and Perry's solution of utilizing predator drones along the border provided more laughter and applause from the audience than when Congressman Ron Paul suggested that a man die because he couldn't afford health care in an earlier debate. But to be fair, the GOP candidates are not solely to blame for the use of the term "illegal." CNN moderator Anderson Cooper used it during the debate, and President Obama has used the term himself, especially early in his presidency, to appease those on the right.

As of March, 16 state legislatures had introduced legislation mirroring Arizona's SB 1070, which essentially legalized racial profiling against undocumented immigrants. (8) In Arizona, journalists have asked Governor Jan Brewer the million-dollar question: What does an illegal immigrant look like? They have yet to get an answer, but for many he or she is Latino. As the "illegal" rhetoric dehumanizes millions of U.S. residents, anti-immigrant sentiment continues to rise, and Latinos are the primary focus of the immigration backlash.

"[A]nti-Latino hate crimes rose disproportionately to other hate crimes between 2004 and 2008," wrote Cristina Costantini, the Associate Editor of *The Huffington Post's* Latino Voices, in October. She cited a congressionally mandated National Institute of Justice study, which estimated that hate crimes against Latinos rose from 426 in 2003, to 595 in 2007. "According to the same study, California and Texas saw the most anti-Latino hate crimes, as well as more dramatic increases of such incidents than any other state," she wrote. (9)

The reality is even more disturbing. According to Mark Potok, a spokesperson for the SPLC: "Latinos, and in particular undocumented immigrants, are among the least likely to report hate crimes because they fear deportation." (10)

Not all immigrant groups are quite so vulnerable. Although the Irish once suffered tremendously at the hands of those who believed they too were not entitled to their basic human rights in the United States, there status has now improved. In New York City, where thousands of undocumented Irish immigrants continue to settle, it appears that the illegal immigration rhetoric does little to affect the success or failure of the Irish today.

Irish Central, the largest Irish-American media site in the United States, recently found that undocumented Irish, unlike many of their Latino counterparts, actually have little trouble adjusting to their new lives in New York City.

"It is so good for many Irish in New York City that in some cases, many find jobs without having to prove the worker has a visa!" wrote Irish Central contributor Ines Novacic in early October. "Several said it's far easier for them to work illegally in New York City than other nationalities." (11) According to James O'Malley, an immigration lawyer from Ireland and the head of the Manhattan-based O'Malley and Associates firm, overall immigration from Ireland in the first half of 2011 was up 12% compared to last year.

This reality simply highlights the racist undertones of the immigration debate, where undocumented white Europeans are embraced by society and Latinos are criminalized, detained, deported, and shunned. In the past few years, there have been successful campaigns against those who ignite racially charged and bigoted statements against the immigrant population. A few years ago, several national advocacy organizations, like the National Council of La Raza (NCLR)—a civil rights group representing 300 affiliates nation wide—launched the successful Drop Dobbs campaign against CNN host Lou Dobbs. This effort focused on encouraging advertisers to no longer support The Lou Dobbs Show. Dobbs hosted a nightly program with a focus on U.S. immigration. On top of his own anti-immigrant rhetoric, he allowed guests with similar views to publicly make statements that ignited, what the NCLR, Media Matters, and the SLPC called, "a toxic climate in our communities." If this was not enough to provoke a response from these advocacy groups, Dobbs later broadcasted his radio show from Capitol Hill as part of FAIRS anti-immigrant "Hold Their Feet to the Fire" lobbying conference and rally. (12) The Drop Dobbs campaign was so successful that in 2009 CNN released him from his duties as a primetime host and his show was canceled.

To some, the term "illegal" is not a big deal. For many the use of the term "undocumented" and other similar words is just a way of being politically correct, tip-toeing around the issue. But the use of the term "illegal" in the U.S. media is biased and racist, preventing any progress in the discussion of immigration reform. It is a rallying cry for hate groups who see undocumented immigrants as parasites on the fabric of the country. As the debate on immigration increases, so will anti-immigrant legislation and anti-Latino rhetoric. While undocumented immigrants are representative in every group in the United States, Latinos are increasingly affected. According to the Pew Hispanic Center, the Latino population accounted for 56% of the nation's growth, from 2000 to 2010. (13) The only way to have a constructive discussion about the issue of immigration, and to find a solution to our broken system, is through a massive restructuring of our way of thinking, in particular the language we use to define a human being. In this process, the media—like it or not—has a significant role to play.

"Elevating our country's conversation on immigration means focusing less on the often angry, overheated rhetoric coming from groups such as the Minuteman Project," wrote Vargas in late September, and instead telling the stories of those "who are aiding undocumented immigrants ... to address an issue that the federal government has not." (14)

1. Do you think the term "illegal" is acceptable because it is honest and direct (as some claim)? Or do you think the term is potentially biased and hateful, and therefore should be avoided?

2. In general, how important do you think names, labels, and terms are in fueling political discourse? Is "undocumented" just another politically correct term? Or does it reflect a desire to humanize migrants?

"HAS ARIZONA'S ECONOMY IMPROVED BECAUSE OF ITS IMMIGRATION LAWS?" BY ANTHONY CAVE, FROM POLITIFACT ARIZONA IN PARTNERSHIP WITH ABC ARIZONA, MARCH 3, 2016

Texas Sen. Ted Cruz has talked tough on immigration, saying he would deport all 12 million undocumented immigrants.

CNN's Wolf Blitzer asked Cruz what is wrong with letting the "good ones" come back to the United States during the Feb. 25 GOP debate in Houston.

Cruz referenced a Feb. 9 *Wall Street Journal* article and said Arizona's strict immigration laws have prompted undocumented immigrants to flee the state. As a result, it has become tougher for business owners in the state to find skilled workers, but at the same time state spending decreased.

"Arizona put in very tough laws on illegal immigration, and the result was illegal immigrants fled the state. ... Some of the business owners complained that the wages they had to pay workers went up, and from their perspective that was a bad thing. But what the state of Arizona has seen is the dollars they're spending on welfare, on prisons, and education, all of those have dropped by hundreds of millions of dollars," Cruz said. "And, the Americans, and for that matter, the legal immigrants who are in Arizona, are seeing unemployment drop, are seeing wages rise. That's who we need to be fighting for."

Arizona is no stranger to controversy with some of its immigration laws. But has the departure of undocumented immigrants after legislation helped Arizona's economy to the tune of hundreds of millions of dollars?

We decided to fact-check Cruz's complex immigration claim.

But first, some background on Arizona immigration policy.

WHY DID IMMIGRANTS LEAVE?

Arizona's undocumented immigrant population was on the climb prior to 2007, according to a Pew Research Center study. The population peaked in 2007 with about 500,000 undocumented immigrants in-state.

But from 2007 to 2012, the undocumented immigrant population dropped 40 percent. However, immigrants across the state were already leaving because of the December 2007 recession.

Arizona's housing market crashed and construction jobs, one of the state's major sectors, dried up.

Immigrants "have left long before the passage of these anti-immigration laws," said Lisa Magaña, an associate professor in the School of Transborder Studies at Arizona State University.

Arizona passed Proposition 200 in 2004, which requires citizenship to receive social services such as childcare and housing assistance.

The state passed Proposition 300 two years later, which bars in-state tuition for college students without a lawful immigration status.

But the meat of Arizona's policies toward undocumented immigrants did not start until 2008.

Arizona required employers to use the federal E-Verify system in 2008, which requires an employee to have a Social Security number to legally work.

Finally, then-Gov. Jan Brewer signed SB 1070 into law in April 2010. The measure allowed law enforcement officers with "reasonable suspicion" to ask for a person's immigration papers when engaging in a stop. Most of the law was struck down by the U.S. Supreme Court, but last September a U.S. District Court Judge upheld the law's provision that allows police to question the immigration status of those they suspect are undocumented.

WELFARE

Welfare has "never gone" to undocumented immigrants, Liz Schott, a senior fellow and welfare expert at the left-leaning Center on Budget and Policy Priorities, said.

However, some children of undocumented immigrants are eligible for benefits if they were born in the United States and are citizens.

Steven Camarota, director of research at the Center for Immigration Studies, which favors reduced immigration, noted that these U.S.-born children could share their cash welfare benefits with their undocumented parents.

In 2008, Arizona spent more than $121 million in cash welfare. In 2014, they spent more than $32 million on cash welfare.

According to Schott, Arizona just spends more in other welfare areas, such as child-care assistance for those working and/or attending school.

"They're spending it all, they're just spending it elsewhere," Schott said.

Because it is difficult to determine how many undocumented immigrants receive cash welfare, it's hard to credit this drop to people leaving the state.

PRISONS

As for state prisons, Arizona's Department of Corrections tracks noncitizens, either documented or undocumented, with a felony conviction.

From fiscal year 2010, which ran from July 2009 to June 2010, to fiscal year 2015, the state's noncitizen prison population has declined almost 23 percent, but that's just about 1,400 inmates.

The daily cost of keeping a noncitizen in a state prison hasn't changed much, either.

In fiscal year 2010, it cost $59.85 per day to house a noncitizen. In fiscal year 2015, it cost $61.55. Because of the dip in noncitizen inmates, that's a savings of almost $28 million.

However, overall state spending on prisons has increased almost 17 percent between 2008 and 2015.

Elliott Pollack, CEO of his own Scottsdale-based economic consulting firm, said Cruz's rationale bothers him.

"The cause and effect might be there to some extent, but I just don't see how it saves hundreds of millions of dollars," Pollack said. "There's no evidence of that."

Meanwhile, Camarota said the departure of undocumented immigrants "makes things a little better."

"Could he (Cruz) be right? He could be," Camarota said.

However, Cruz's points are subject to error. Camarota also notes that undocumented immigrants "paid something" in taxes.

A February 2016 report from the left-leaning Institute on Taxation and Economic Policy estimates that Arizona's undocumented immigrants pay more than $231 million a year in state and local taxes.

EDUCATION

On education, the state also does not track spending on undocumented immigrants in schools.

The *Wall Street Journal* article Cruz described uses the state's decline in intensive English student enrollment —about 80,000 students between 2008 and 2012—as a potential cost-saving measure, noting that it could save the state about $350 million per year.

But it's not that simple.

"I think it's a combination of factors," Arizona Department of Education spokesman Charles Tack said, noting that the decline could be attributed to students leaving the system or being reclassified elsewhere.

Plus, that measure correlates intensive English with undocumented immigrants, which isn't tracked to begin with.

We reached out to the Cruz campaign for comment but did not hear back.

OUR RULING

Cruz said, "spending on welfare, on prisons, and education, all of those have dropped by hundreds of millions of dollars" because of Arizona's exodus of undocumented immigrants.

That's far from clear.

While it's technically possible to receive cash welfare through U.S.-born children, undocumented immigrants do not receive cash welfare directly. And, the state's prison and education budgets do not solely account for those without papers.

Even then, any potential savings would be hard to calculate. It is not an apples to oranges comparison.

The recession played a significant role in Arizona's immigrant population decline, too. There's been no noticeable windfall in the state budget for welfare, education and prisons that we could document.

We rate Cruz's claim as Mostly False.

1. Why would politicians such as Cruz make such claims about the costs of immigration that are not rooted in fact? What benefit might they provide?

CHAPTER 6

WHAT ORDINARY PEOPLE SAY

As we know, the familiar mythology of an America "built by immigrants" glosses over the eradication of Native Americans and the forced immigration of African slaves—among other unresolved social conflicts. Still, perhaps due to the grain of truth in the American origin story, most citizens do not openly embrace extreme reactionary views on immigration. Although politicians on the right stoke xenophobic flames with untenable plans to build a wall, the majority of Americans do not support these views, either in theory or in practice. Most see immigration as beneficial to America, with the caveat that it should be done through the proper legal channels.

According to the Pew Research Center, polls reveal that six out of ten respondents favor a path to citizenship for those already residing in the country. This percentage increases if a path to permanent residence is included. Only 17 percent of the public support deportation for those currently in the country illegally.

Our relationship to refugees is somewhat different. Although we pay lip service to humanitarian efforts, refugees have typically been a canvas upon which Americans project distrust of a foreign "other." The face of this political bogeyman changes with the times. But is our fear of potential terrorists among Syrian refugees much different that our suspicion of communist spies hiding among the Hungarian refugees of sixty years ago?

Above all, our opinion of those seeking to become Americans is marked by ambivalence: Obama has deported record numbers while at the same time pursuing executive action on behalf of immigrants. And we fear refugees fleeing ISIS might themselves be terrorists. Thus, a nuanced understanding of immigration and refugees on a case-by-case basis is essential if we wish to avoid dangerous and potentially discriminatory confusion.

"WHAT AMERICANS WANT TO DO ABOUT ILLEGAL IMMIGRATION," BY SARA KEHAULANI GOO, FROM THE PEW RESEARCH CENTER, AUGUST 24, 2015

The debate over the future of the nation's estimated 11.3 million unauthorized immigrants is on the political front burner once more.

President Barack Obama set the stage in November when he announced new executive actions (now tied up in court) to prevent the deportation of millions of unauthorized immigrants, expanding 2012's original program aimed mostly at providing relief to those brought to the United States as children. Illegal immigration has dominated the Republican presidential campaign, particularly after Donald Trump's call for deporting all undocumented immigrants in the U.S. and building a wall along the U.S.-Mexico border. Others have called for a changing the constitutional amendment that guarantees birthright citizenship.

Among the public overall, there is little support for an effort to deport all those in the U.S. illegally, but surveys in past years have found greater support for building a barrier along the Mexican border and for changing the Constitution to ban birthright citizenship.

Republicans have long been conflicted over U.S. immigration policy. On the one hand, consistent majorities of Republicans favor providing a path to legal status for people in the U.S. illegally. Yet most Republicans also worry that granting legal status to undocumented immigrants would amount to a tacit reward for illegal behavior.

And in the past, nearly half of Republicans supported changing the Constitution to bar birthright citizenship, and a majority supported building a fence along the entire U.S. border with Mexico.

Here's a breakdown of public opinion on some key immigration issues:

Stay or deport? In a Pew Research Center survey conducted in May, a solid majority (72%) of Americans – including 80% of Democrats, 76% of independents and 56% of Republicans – say undocumented immigrants currently living in the U.S. should be allowed to stay in this country legally if they meet certain requirements. Last year, we asked a follow-up question of those who opposed granting legal status to undocumented immigrants: Should there be a "national law enforcement effort to deport" all immigrants here illegally? Just 17% of the public overall favored such an effort, including about a quarter (27%) of Republicans.

Moreover, in a 2013 survey, 76% of Republicans said that deporting all immigrants in the U.S. illegally was "unrealistic."

One measure of public sentiment is how Americans have felt about the record number of deportations of unauthorized immigrants during the Obama administration – and an early-2014 survey found the public was divided. Overall, 45% of Americans called the increase in such deportations a good thing and the same share said it was a bad thing. Republicans (55% good thing), especially Republicans and Republican leaners who agree with the Tea Party (65%), were more likely than Democrats (37%) to have a positive view of increased deportations.

A majority (60%) of Hispanics saw the increase in deportations as a bad thing. In another survey of Latino adults in 2013, nearly half (46%) said they worry "a lot" or "some" that they, a family member or a close friend could be deported. And 56% said it was more important for undocumented immigrants to be able to work and live in the U.S. without the threat of deportation than to obtain a pathway to citizenship, according to our 2014 poll.

Birthright citizenship: One of the proposals raised in the current Republican presidential campaign is whether to change the U.S. Constitution's 14th Amendment, which states, "All persons born or naturalized in the United States, and subject to the jurisdiction thereof, are citizens of the United States and of the State wherein they reside." On that issue, a majority of Americans (57%) in February 2011 said that the Constitution should remain as it is, allowing any child born in the U.S. full citizenship; 39% favored changing the Constitution to bar birthright citizenship. (Also, we found that 87% of Americans were aware of this birthright.)

At that time, the idea of ending birthright citizenship drew broad opposition among Hispanics (73%), young people (73% of those under 30) and Democrats (66%). However, Republicans were divided: 49% wanted to leave the Constitution as it is, while 47% favored a constitutional amendment to bar birthright citizenship.

In 2012, at least 4.5 million U.S.-born children lived with at least one unauthorized parent, according to our analysis. Some 4 million unauthorized immigrant adults lived with their U.S.-born children.

Build a wall, or a fence: Our most recent survey on this issue was in October 2011. At that time, 46% favored building a fence "along the entire border with Mexico," while 47% were opposed. Republicans (62%) were far more likely than independents (44%) or Democrats (39%) to support the construction of a border fence.

Overall views of immigrants: Views about immigration policies are often shaped by views about immigrants themselves: Are immigrants generally a problem, taking jobs and services, or do they strengthen the country through hard work and talents?

In our May survey, about half of Americans (51%) say immigrants strengthen the country, while 41% view them as a burden. (These opinions have fluctuated over the years, but in the mid-1990s, majorities said immigrants to the U.S. were a burden.) However, Republicans (63%) are far more likely than Democrats (32%) to say immigrants are a burden. And the share of Republicans who regard immigrants as a burden jumped 15 percentage points, from 48% in March 2014.

Declining immigration: The latest immigration debate comes against a backdrop in which the number of unauthorized immigrants coming to the U.S. has leveled off. That number peaked in 2007, especially for those from Mexico.

As growth of this group has stalled, there has been a recent sharp rise in the median length of time that unauthorized immigrants have lived in the U.S. In 2013, unauthorized immigrant adults had been in the U.S. for a median time of nearly 13 years – meaning that half had been in the country at least that long, according to a preliminary estimate. A decade earlier, in 2003, the median for adults was less than eight years.

Despite the renewed focus on immigration, it's worth keeping in mind that immigration has not ranked high in our annual poll on the issues Americans see as a top priority for the president and Congress. Even among Hispanics, immigration has not been a top priority; a 2014 survey found that Hispanics rated education (92%), jobs and the economy (91%), and health care (86%) as extremely or very important issues but fewer said the same about immigration (73%).

1. This article states that a large majority of Americans support a path to citizenship for immigrants currently in the United States. What do you think?

"AMERICA HAS NEVER ACTUALLY WELCOMED THE WORLD'S HUDDLED MASSES," BY MARIA CRISTINA GARCIA, FROM *THE WASHINGTON POST,* NOVEMBER 21, 2015

For a growing number of politicians, this month's attacks in Paris mean it's time to stop bringing Syrian refugees to the United States. The risk that the Islamic State might send infiltrators in disguise, the theory goes, outweighs America's usual attitude toward taking in desperate people from around the world. "Our nation has always been welcoming, but we cannot let terrorists take advantage of our compassion," House Speaker Paul D. Ryan, R-Wisconsin, said Tuesday. "This is a moment where it's better to be safe than to be sorry." By the middle of this past week, more than half the country's governors had declared that their states wouldn't accept any resettled Syrians. Things had changed after Paris.

In truth, they hadn't. The outcry over resettling a relatively small number of Syrian refugees—far fewer than France vowed to take in even after the attacks—isn't an exception; it's more like the rule. Yes, the United States has been generous: Since 1948, close to 4 million refugees have come here. But despite our reputation as a haven for the oppressed, those admissions have always been controversial. There is one way the Syrian refugees are different, though: They, and others who have arrived after 9/11, are among the most carefully vetted in American history.

U.S. refugee policy dates to the end of World War II. During the 1930s and 1940s, the nation turned away thousands of Jews fleeing the Third Reich, even though our immigration quotas remained unfilled. Politicians justified their actions by arguing that German spies and subversives might be hiding among the refugees, but anti-Semitism was the more likely motivation for American neglect.

After the war, President Harry S. Truman and his allies on Capitol Hill urged Congress to authorize the admission of displaced and stateless people from Europe. Financial aid to war-torn nations was not enough, they argued; the United States had a moral obligation to accept a share of the refugees. Even as Americans became more fully aware of the horrors of the Nazi death camps, Congress resisted. It took three years to pass the 1948 Displaced Persons Act, which brought in more than 200,000 Europeans (mostly ethnic Germans) over the next two years. The law discriminated against Jewish and Catholic refugees, and Truman was tempted to veto it because it was "wholly inconsistent with the American sense of justice." Still, the law officially launched U.S. refugee policy. Together with the 1953 Refugee Relief Act, it facilitated the entry of almost 600,000 European refugees.

In 1956, President Dwight Eisenhower had to convince a wary American public that it was in the national interest to accept Hungarian refugees. A Hungarian rebellion against Soviet domination had elicited a brutal crackdown that forced more than 200,000 refugees into Austria and Yugoslavia and destabilized two countries still reeling from World War II. Opponents argued that communist spies and saboteurs would arrive with the refugee flow and harm the nation. Supporters said the United States had a moral responsibility to the Hungarian rebels and to the European host nations—especially since the U.S. government had encouraged the rebellion through propaganda broadcasts on Radio Free Europe.

The Eisenhower administration enlisted the help of public relations firms to generate positive press for the refugee program and "sell" the Hungarians to the public. For the next year, Americans were subjected to a massive media blitz, with story after story on Hungarian freedom fighters, comparing them to American patriots and stressing their love of liberty and democracy. Eventually, 38,000 Hungarians were admitted, many of them screened and registered at Camp Kilmer, New Jersey.

Subsequent groups faced similar backlashes. The 200,000 Cubans who were paroled into the United States from 1959 to 1962 after Fidel Castro's rise to power were predominantly white, middle-class and professionally trained, but that did little to pacify Americans, especially those living in South Florida, who bore the brunt of the refugee crisis. While the national media celebrated the refugees' heroism and "American" values (one *Newsweek* story enthusiastically told readers, "They're OK!"), letters to politicians and civic leaders revealed growing anger and frustration in Miami. Over the next five decades, South Florida residents would see many more refugees from Cuba - through the freedom flights from 1965 to 1973, the 1980 Mariel boatlift and the attempts in 1994 by more than 30,000 Cubans to flee by boat - as well as arrivals from Haiti, Nicaragua, Venezuela and Colombia. Today, Miami is home to one of the most successful Latino business communities in the nation, but the demographic shift scared away many non-Hispanic white residents, who resented the cultural transformation of "their" city.

Polls in the 1970s found opposition to the continued entry of Vietnamese refugees and other Southeast Asians fleeing the devastating war in Vietnam and its aftermath. News stories about the high casualty rates of Vietnamese boat people stranded at sea and about squalid refugee camps in Thailand did little to change public opinion: By 1979, only 32 percent of Americans surveyed wanted to accommodate more Southeast Asian refugees, and the government struggled to find people willing to sponsor them. Americans complained that the refugees were culturally "unassimilable," politically suspect, self-interested migrants who came to mooch off the welfare system. Resentment fueled conflict in many communities across the country, from Philadelphia to Port Arthur, Texas, to Los Angeles.

Cuba and Vietnam (along with the Soviet Union) eventually became the top source countries of refugees during the Cold War. As in the Hungarian case, the White House took the lead in crafting refugee policy, so much so that Congress passed the 1980 Refugee Act to make admissions more accountable to public will. Since then, the White House, in consultation with Congress, has established an annual refugee quota, with numbers allotted to different regions of the world. These allotments reflect geopolitical and foreign policy interests, as well as humanitarian obligations.

But 9/11 completely changed our refugee policy. In the wake of the terrorist attacks, the George W. Bush administration restructured the immigration bureaucracy to convey a greater sense of safety to the public. Refugee admissions were casualties of that restructuring. The annual quota constantly goes unfilled; 2013 marked the closest we came to meeting it after 9/11, although even before then, the quota was almost never met. Refugees now face many bureaucratic hurdles: They must be investigated by national and international intelligence agencies; their fingerprints and other biometric data are checked against terrorist and criminal databases. They are screened for disease. They are interviewed and rein-terviewed by consular officials. In sum, they must prove that they are worthy of refuge in the United States.

The State Department reports that refugee appli-cants can expect to wait on average 18 to 24 months for processing and screening, but humanitarian aid workers on the ground report a much longer wait. Just like other immigrants, refugee applicants are not guar-anteed admission. There is no "waiting list" per se, and the selection process can be capricious. Even Iraqi and Afghan translators, already cleared to work with

U.S. military personnel, have difficulty securing refugee status or special immigrant visas. If many in this doubly vetted population can't get visas, those without connections will encounter still greater obstacles.

This past week's political rhetoric warns that the Syrian refugee population, dominated by young men traveling alone, poses a risk. But adult males traveling solo are the least likely to be admitted to the United States unless they can demonstrate persecution. U.S. resettlement policies favor women and children, the elderly and the infirm, victims of torture, and religious minorities. Those with family here are also prioritized.

As generous as our refugee policy has been, the real burden is borne by countries that border areas of crisis. The Zaatari refugee camp in Jordan, near the Syrian border, for instance, is home to 80,000 people. The U.N. High Commissioner for Refugees refers only 1 percent of refugees for resettlement in third countries such as the United States. The refugees our nation admits each year are but a drop in the proverbial bucket.

In September, the Obama administration announced that it would increase the annual refugee quota over the next two years to accommodate a larger number of Syrians. The quota, set at 70,000 to 80,000 for more than a decade now, will increase to 100,000 by October 2017. This will be the largest refugee quota since before 9/11. But the numbers are allotted by region, not country, and Syrians compete for visas with many other displaced people. In 2012, amid Syrian President Bashar Assad's violent crackdown, only 31 Syrian refugees were admitted to the United States. This year, despite the ongoing civil war and the rise of the Islamic State, just 1,682 refugees came from Syria - 2.4 percent of the total refugee admissions. The administration promises that at least 10,000 of the coming year's 85,000 refugees will be Syrian, but the numbers will probably be smaller.

Is it possible that a terrorist will arrive undetected in the small pool of admitted refugees? No system is 100 percent secure. Even tourism can pose a potential threat: The Tsarnaev brothers, responsible for the Boston Marathon bombing, arrived in the United States on tourist visas in 2002 and became legal residents when their parents were granted asylum. So it was the asylum bureaucracy, not the refugee system, that handled their case. But what immigration official can predict that children will be radicalized on American soil?

So some fears and suspicions are understandable. But we can't always protect ourselves from our homegrown assassins, either. (Who predicted Columbine, Sandy Hook, Charleston?) We live in a society unable to guarantee safety on our streets and our college campuses, in our movie theaters, churches and schools.

Sixty years ago, Eisenhower reminded the nation that the United States must accept its "full share" in assisting victims of oppression. That remains true. Denying vulnerable populations—and populations we made vulnerable—the chance to make a case for refuge goes against everything our country claims to stand for. If fear paralyzes our movements, dictates our policies and erases a proud humanitarian tradition, then those who wish us harm will celebrate indeed.

1. Do you think our current screening process can prevent all potential terrorists from sneaking through as refugees? Is the risk high or low, in your opinion?

2. What steps should those who support refugee resettlement take to change public opinion?

"OVER THE DECADES, AMERICAN PUBLIC GENERALLY HASN'T WELCOMED REFUGEES," BY DREW DESILVER, FROM THE PEW RESEARCH CENTER, NOVEMBER 19, 2015

Last week's Islamic State attacks in Paris have heightened concerns about possible security threats posed by the hundreds of thousands of Middle Eastern refugees pouring into Europe. And Europeans aren't the only ones concerned: Opposition is building in the U.S. to the Obama administration's plans to admit up to 10,000 refugees from Syria's civil war.

A new Bloomberg Politics poll found that 53% of Americans don't want to accept any Syrian refugees at all; 11% more would accept only Christian refugees from Syria. More than two dozen governors, most of them Republicans, have said they'll oppose Syrian refugees being resettled in their states. And on Thursday the House of Representatives passed a bill blocking the admission of Syrian and Iraqi refugees unless they pass strict background checks.

The U.S. cap on refugee admissions was raised to 85,000 this fiscal year from 70,000 in fiscal 2015, largely to accommodate the planned increase in Syrian refugees and, more broadly, help deal with the influx of hundreds of thousands of migrants from that country, Iraq, Afghanistan and elsewhere into Europe. In a Pew Research Center survey taken in September, Americans narrowly approved of that policy shift (51% to 45%), though it's unknown whether public opinion has shifted after the Paris attacks.

A look back into the opinion-polling archives (courtesy of Cornell's Roper Center for Public Opinion Research) shows that American opposition to admitting large numbers of foreigners fleeing war and oppression has been pretty consistent, regardless of official government policy. We examined instances over the past eight decades where large groups of refugees from specific countries or regions were seeking admission, typically above and beyond the immigration rules in place at the time, and for which there was reliable polling data. Here's what we found:

BEFORE AND AFTER WORLD WAR II

In the years leading up to the Second World War, as has been noted elsewhere, large majorities of Americans opposed allowing refugees from European dictatorships to come to the United States. In 1938, the polling firm Roper found that 67% opposed "German, Austrian and other political refugees" coming to the U.S., versus 18% who would allow them to come and 5% who would encourage them to come. In 1939, a Gallup poll found similar opposition when it asked more specifically about support for "10,000 refugee children from Germany" coming to the United States.

The war uprooted millions of Europeans from their homes; by the end of 1947 there were still an estimated 800,000 "displaced persons." Some U.S. governors with declining populations in their states said there was room for refugees, but public attitudes remained less than welcoming: In a 1948 Gallup poll, for example, 57% said they would disapprove of any plans to resettle about 10,000 displaced Europeans in their state.

Nonetheless, in 1948 Congress passed the Displaced Persons Act, which authorized the entry of 200,000 (later raised to 415,000) European refugees above normal immigration quotas. By the end of 1952, just over 400,000 people – mostly from Eastern Europe and the Soviet Union – had been admitted under the law.

HUNGARY, 1950S

After Soviet troops crushed the Hungarian uprising of 1956, nearly 200,000 Hungarians fled to Austria and Yugoslavia. In July 1958, Gallup asked what Americans thought about a suggestion that 65,000 Hungarian refugees be allowed to resettle in the U.S. Although Cold War tensions were running high, more than half (55%) disapproved of the idea, with only 33% approving of it. In the end, 30,752 Hungarians were admitted under the Hungarian Refugee Act of 1958.

INDOCHINA, 1970S

Following the final collapse of South Vietnam in 1975, the U.S. evacuated some 130,000 Indochinese – Vietnamese, Cambodians and Laotians – fleeing the new Communist government. Americans were deeply divided on whether these refugees should be allowed to live in the United States: In a May 1975 Harris poll, for example, 37% were in favor, 49% opposed, and 14% weren't sure. Nonetheless, the refugees were allowed to stay.

Later in the decade, hundreds of thousands of people living in Vietnam (including many ethnic Chinese) began leaving the country in overcrowded boats. At the same time, thousands of Cambodians and Laotians were escaping their countries over land. In response to the humanitarian crisis, President Jimmy Carter in June 1979 doubled the number of Indochinese refugees the U.S. had previously agreed to accept, to 14,000 a month. The move was not popular: In a CBS News/New York Times poll the following month, 62% disapproved of Carter's action. But between 1980 and 1990, according to federal immigration data compiled by Pew Research Center, nearly 590,000 refugees from Vietnam, Cambodia and Laos were admitted into the U.S.

CUBA IN 1980 AND HAITI IN 1994

The United States experienced its own "boat people" phenomenon in 1980, when the Cuban government allowed tens of thousands of people to leave the island in what became known as the Mariel boatlift. By the time the boatlift ended in late October that year, some 125,000

Cubans had arrived in south Florida. Under U.S. law governing Cuban emigrants, the refugees were allowed to stay once they reached U.S. soil.

The boatlift was not popular among Americans, particularly after media reports that criminals and mental patients were among the refugees (though ultimately only about 2,700, or 2.2%, were returned to Cuba). In a June 1980 CBS/New York Times poll, 71% said they disapproved allowing the Cubans to settle in the U.S.

A second wave of Cuban emigration to the U.S. occurred in 1994, accompanied by several thousand Haitians fleeing that country's political turmoil and grinding poverty. Public opinion on these migrations was even more negative: In a September 1994 CBS/New York Times poll, large majorities disapproved of letting the refugees settle in the U.S. – 80% vs. 15% approval in the case of the Cubans, 77% vs. 19% in the case of the Haitians. The official U.S. response was very different from in 1980: More than 30,000 Cubans and 20,000 Haitians were intercepted at sea and interned at the U.S. base at Guantanamo Bay. Most of the Cubans eventually were admitted to the U.S., but only about half the Haitians were, according to a Brookings Institution report.

KOSOVO, 1999

During the 1998-99 war between what was left of Yugoslavia and the Kosovo Liberation Army, roughly a million Kosovars – half the territory's population – were either refugees in neighboring countries or internally displaced. In April 1999, as part of a multinational response to the crisis, the U.S. agreed to accept up to 20,000 Kosovar refugees. Public opinion on the move was split but more favorable toward taking the refugees than in previous crises: In a CBS/New York Times poll taken that month, 40% said accepting the refugees was the right thing for the U.S. to do, 31% said the U.S. should do less, and 19% said the U.S. should do more. In the end, according to State Department data, just over 14,000 Kosovars were admitted into the country.

In 2013, the number of migrants worldwide was estimated at over 230 million.[1] As we move further into the twenty-

1. Looking back on history, it seems most refugees were scapegoats of whatever political bogeyman existed at the time. Do you think Syrian refugees fit into this pattern, or do ISIS and a new paradigm of terror make refugees from this region a realistic threat to US security?

2. Do you notice any overarching patterns and relationship between US foreign policy and refugees? Should the United States be accountable to victims of political unrest caused, in part, by American intervention in foreign affairs? Or is this irrelevant to humanitarian concerns?

CONCLUSION

first century, we can expect these numbers to rise. There are many reasons behind this projected increase, primary among them being inept US interventions with no long-term strategy and an increasing number of war-torn and failed states, particularly in the Middle East. From Syria alone, the amount of refugees generated by a complex civil war is almost five million. Add to these numbers the many millions in the coming decades who will be displaced by sea-level rises associated with climate change, and it is fair to say that a migration and refugee crisis may become this century's defining characteristic.

This reality will likely strain the international community's ability to handle the situation. Presently, Europe is absorbing the majority of global migration due to its location. However, even in response to migration that can be covered with current resources, some European nations, such as Hungary, are experiencing a xenophobic backlash. Other nations, including Germany, have welcomed migrants and refugees in great numbers, although how well these groups will function economically and culturally within the German nation remains an open question.

Although the United States is shielded from much migration due to geography, we can expect immigration to increase to the point that no ethnicity will hold a majority by 2065.[2] While far-right politicians may suggest stopping this with a wall, this is not, in fact, a practical solution. To those who argue that immigrants depress wages, one might reply that common ground can be found between the native born and immigrant worker, and that interests promoting wealth inequality might be the common foe. To see past "divide and conquer" rhetoric that only helps the powerful few, a contextualized view of immigration is critical—we hope the articles collected herein have provided just this.

BIBLIOGRAPHY

Anft, Michael. "Giving a Voice to Hispanics." *Chronicle of Philanthropy,* Jan. 20, 2005. Business Collection. Web. Dec. 19, 2015.

Cafaro, Philip. "The Progressive Case for Reducing Immigration." *The Chronicle of Higher Education* 61.19 (2015). General OneFile. Web. Dec. 17, 2015.

Cave, Anthony. "Fact Check: Ted Cruz Claims Arizona's Immigration Laws Helped Economy." PolitiFact and ABC Arizona, March 3, 2016. Retrieved May 17, 2016 (http://www.politifact. com/arizona/statements/2016/mar/03/ted-cruz/has-arizonas-economy-improved-because-its-immigrat).

Cohen, D'vera. "Future Immigration Will Change the Face of America by 2065." Pew Research Center, October 5, 2015. Retrieved May 17, 2016 (http://www.pewresearch.org/fact-tank/2015/10/05/future-immigration-will-change-the-face-of-america-by-2065).

Edwards, Adrian. "UNHCR Viewpoint: 'Refugee' or 'Migrant' – Which is Right?" UN Refugee Agency, August 27, 2015. Retrieved May 17, 2016 (http://www.unhcr.org/55df0e556.html).

Eichenwald, Kurt. "Illegal Immigration: Myths, Half-Truths and a Hole in Trump's Wall." *Newsweek*, October 23, 2015. General OneFile. Web. Dec. 17, 2015.

Garcia, Maria Cristina. "America Has Never Actually Welcomed the World's Huddled Masses." *Washington Post,* November 21, 2015. Retrieved January 13, 2016 (https://www.washingtonpost. com/opinions/america-has-never-actually-welcomed-the-worlds-huddled-masses/2015/11/20/6763fad0-8e71-11e5-ae1f-af46b7df8483_story.html).

Goo, Sara Kehaulani. "What Americans Want to Do About Illegal Immigration." Pew Research Center, August 24, 2015. Retrieved May 17, 2016 (http://www.pewresearch.org/fact-tank/2015/08/24/what-americans-want-to-do-about-illegal-immigration).

"In Mixed Ruling, Supreme Court Overturns Parts of Arizona's S.B. 1070, Upholds 'Show Me Your Papers.'" *Democracy Now!*, June 26, 2012. Retrieved May 17, 2016 (http://www.democracynow.org/2012/6/26/in_mixed_ruling_supreme_court_overturns).

Joseph, Matthew H. "*Immigration and Naturalization Service v. Elias-Zacarias:* Partially Closing the Door on Political Asylum." *The Maryland Law Review* 52:2 (1993).

Krikorian, Mark. "The Syrian Refugee Crisis and Its Impact on the Security of the U.S. Refugee Admissions Program." Testimony before the US House of Representatives, November 2015. Retrieved May 17, 2016 from (https://judiciary.house.gov/wp-content/uploads/2016/02/11.19.15-Hetfield-Testimony.pdf).

Lazare, Sarah. "'Wrong Side of History': Outrage as US Congress Moves to Block Syrian Refugees." *Common Dreams*, November 18, 2015. Retrieved May 17, 2016 (http://www.commondreams.org/news/2015/11/18/wrong-side-history-outrage-us-congress-moves-block-syrian-refugees).

Makwana, Rajesh. "The Global Refugee Crisis: Humanity's Last Call for a Culture of Sharing and Cooperation." *Common Dreams,* March 15, 2016. Retrieved May 17, 2016 (http://www.commondreams.org/views/2016/03/15/global-refugee-crisis-humanitys-last-call-culture-sharing-and-cooperation).

McCaul, Michael T. "Letter to President Obama from the Committee on Homeland Security." US House of Representatives Committee on Homeland Security, June 11, 2015. Retrieved May 17, 2016 (https://homeland.house.gov/files/documents/061115-Letter-Syrian-Refugee%20States.pdf).

Morin, Rich. "Crime Rises Among Second-Generation Immigrants as They Assimilate." Pew Research Center, October 15, 2013. Retrieved May 17, 2016 (http://www.pewresearch.org/fact-tank/2013/10/15/crime-rises-among-second-generation-immigrants-as-they-assimilate).

"NCAPA Letter to President Obama." Asian Americans Advancing Justice, August 2014. Retrieved January 13, 2016 (http://vwww.advancingequality.org/news-media/publications/ncapa-letter-president-obama-august-2014).

"On the Move: 232 Million Migrants Worldwide." *The Guardian,* September 11, 2013. Retrieved May 17, 2016 (http://www. theguardian.com/news/datablog/2013/sep/11/on-the-move-232-million-migrants-in-the-world).

"Over the Decades, American Public Generally Hasn't Welcomed Refugees." Pew Research Center, November 25, 2015. Retrieved January 13, 2016 (http://www.pewresearch.org/fact-tank/2015/11/19/u-s-public-seldom-has-welcomed-refugees-into-country/).

"An Overview of U.S. Refugee Law and Policy." American Immigration Council, November 18, 2015. Retrieved May 17, 2016 (http://www.immigrationpolicy.org/just-facts/refugees-fact-sheet).

Reed, Judith. "Immigrants as Refugees of the Global Economy: Learning to Teach (About) Today's Migrants." *Multicultural Education* 22.3-4 (2015): 2+. General OneFile. Web. Dec. 16, 2015.

"Remarks by the President in Address to the Nation on Immigration." The White House, November 20, 2014. Retrieved January 13, 2016 (https://www.whitehouse.gov/the-press-office/2014/11/20/remarks-president-address-nation-immigration).

Rivera, John-Michael. "The DREAM Act and Other Mexican (American) Questions." *Phi Kappa Phi Forum* 93.2 (2013): 4+. General OneFile. Web. Dec. 17 2015.

Rotella, Sebastian. "Q&A: Can a Divided Europe Handle the Refugee Crisis?" *ProPublica,* September 14, 2015. Retrieved May 17, 2016 (https://www.propublica.org/article/q-and-a-can-a-divided-europe-handle-the-refugee-crisis).

Rubio, Angelica. "Undocumented, Not illegal: Beyond the Rhetoric of Immigration Coverage." *NACLA Report on the Americas* 44.6 (2011): 50+. General OneFile. Web. Dec. 17 2015.

CHAPTER NOTES

INTRODUCTION

1. "An Overview of U.S. Refugee Law and Policy." American Immigration Council, November 18, 2015. http://www.immigrationpolicy.org/just-facts/refugees-fact-sheet.

CHAPTER 1: WHAT THE EXPERTS AND ACADEMICS SAY

"IMMIGRANTS AS REFUGEES OF THE GLOBAL ECONOMY: LEARNING TO TEACH (ABOUT) TODAY'S MIGRANTS," BY JUDITH REED

REFERENCES

Alexander, J. (2007). *Detained: The New Bedford immigration raid.* (Video recording). Active Vista Media.

Anzaldua, G. (1993). *Friends from the other side = Amigos del otro lado*. San Francisco: Children's Book Press.

Bigelow, B. (2006). *The line between us: Teaching about the border and Mexican immigration.* Milwaukee, WI: Rethinking Schools Ltd.

Bigelow, B., & Peterson, B. (Eds.). (2002). *Rethinking globalization: Teaching for justice in an unjust world*. Milwaukee, WI: Rethinking Schools Ltd.

Bunting, E. (1996). *Going home.* New York: HarperCollins.

Dapon, M. S. (2003). *The hidden face of globalization*. (Video recording). Crowing Rooster Arts/National Labor Committee.

Dorros, A. (1993). *Radio Man = Don Radio.* New York: Harper Collins.

Elya, S. M. (2002). *Home at last.* New York: Lee & Low Books.

Krull, K. (2003). *Harvesting hope: The story of Cesar Chavez.* New York: Harcourt.

Nilsen, U. (2001). *Uprooted: Refugees of the global economy.* (Video recording). National Network for Immigrant and Refugee Rights.

Perez, A. I. (2002). *My diary from here to there = Mi diario de aqui hasta alia cuento*. San Francisco: Children's Book Press.

Smothers, E. F. (2003). *The hard-times jar.* New York: Farrar, Straus & Giroux.

Thomas, J. R. (1994). *Lights on the river.* New York: Hyperion Books for Children.

BIBLIOGRAPHY OF SELECTED CHILDREN'S LITERATURE ON IMMIGRATION AND MIGRANT LABOR

Altman, Linda Jacobs. *Amelia's Road.* New York: Lee & Low books, 1993.

Anzaldua, Gloria. *Friends from the Other Side = Amigos del otro lado.* San Francisco: Children's Book Press, 1993.

Atkin, S. Beth. *Voices from the Fields: Children of Migrant Farmworkers Tell Their Stories.* Boston: Little, Brown & Co., 1993.

Badoe, Adwoa. *Nana's Cold Days.* Toronto, Canada/Berkley, CA: Groundwood Books, 2002.

Bunting, Eve. *A Day's Work.* New York: Clarion Books, 1994.

Bunting, Eve. *Going Home.* New York: HarperCollins Publishers, 1996.

Bunting, Eve. *One Green Apple.* New York: Clarion Books, 2006.

DeFelice, Cynthia C. . *Under the Same Sky.* New York: Farrar, Straus & Giroux, 2003.

Dorros, Arthur. *Isla.* New York: Dutton Children's Books, 1995.

Dorros, Arthur. *Radio Man = Don Radio.* New York: Harper Collins, 1993.

Elya, Susan Middleton. *Home at Last.* New York: Lee & Low Books, 2002.

Garay, Luis. *The Long Road.* Plattsburgh, NY: Tundra Books, 2002.

Hoffman, Mary. *The Color of Home.* New York: Phyllis Fogelman Books, 2002.

Johnston, Tony. *Uncle Rain Cloud.* Watertown, MA.: Charlesbridge, 2000.

Krull, Kathleen. *Harvesting Hope: The Story of Cesar Chavez.* New York: Harcourt, 2003.

Lai, Thanhha. *Inside Out & Back Again.* New York: HarperCollins, 2011.

Mora, Pat. *Tomas and the LibraryLady.* New York: Knopf, 1997.

Perez, Amada Irma. *My Diary from Here to There = Mi diario de aqui hasta alia cuento.* San Francisco: Children's Book Press, 2002.

Perez, L. King. *First Day in Grapes.* New York: Lee & Low Books, 2002.

Smothers, Ethel Footman. *The Hard-Times Jar.* New York: Farrar, Straus and Giroux, 2003.

Thomas, Jane Resh. *Lights on the River.* New York: Hyperion Books for Children, 1994.

Veciana-Suarez, Ana. *Flight to Freedom.* New York: Orchard Books, 2002.

Williams, Karen Lynn. *My Name Is Sangoel.* Grand Rapids, MI: Eerdmans Books for Young Readers, 2009.

CHAPTER 2: WHAT THE GOVERNMENT AND POLITICIANS SAY

"THE DREAM ACT AND OTHER MEXICAN (AMERICAN) QUESTIONS," BY JOHN-MICHAEL RIVERA

For footnotes, go online to www.phikappaphi.org/forum/summer2013.

CHAPTER 3: WHAT THE COURTS AND LEGAL COMMUNITY SAY

"IMMIGRATION AND NATURALIZATION SERVICE V. ELIAS-ZACARIAS: PARTIALLY CLOSING THE DOOR ON POLITICAL ASYLUM," BY MATTHEW H. JOSEPH

Due to the length of these endnotes, we have not included them in this book. For all sources, please see http://digitalcommons. law.umaryland.edu/cgi/viewcontent.cgi?article=2869&context =mlr.

CHAPTER 4: WHAT ADVOCATES AND ADVOCACY ORGANIZATIONS SAY

"THE SYRIAN REFUGEE CRISIS AND ITS IMPACT ON THE SECURITY OF THE U.S. REFUGEE ADMISSIONS PROGRAM," BY MARK KRIKORIAN

1. http://www.cis.org/rush/hearing-syrian-refugees-reassurance-and-storytel...
2. http://www.defenseone.com/management/2015/10/chattanoogas-wake-dhs-wants...
3. http://cis.org/cadman/why-syrian-refugee-vetting-will-be-indisputably-fa...
4. "A separate world", The Buffalo News, September 23, 2002.
5. http://www.washingtontimes.com/news/2015/feb/24/islamist-terror-groups-t...
6. http://www.usatoday.com/story/news/politics/2015/10/23/fbi-comey-isil-do...
7. http://cis.org/911-HowMilitantIslamicTerroristsEntered
8. http://abcnews.go.com/Blotter/al-qaeda-kentucky-us-dozens-terrorists-cou...
9. http://www.nydailynews.com/news/crime/idaho-jury-convicts-uzbek-refugee-...
10. http://news.yahoo.com/bosnians-reject-hatred-wake-terror-financing-case-...
11. http://cis.org/High-Cost-of-Resettling-Middle-Eastern-Refugees
12. http://www.unhcr.org/pages/4f9016576.html

"NCAPA LETTER TO PRESIDENT OBAMA," BY NATIONAL COUNCIL OF ASIAN PACIFIC AMERICANS (NCAPA)

1. Center for American Progress, "Why Immigration is an Asian American Issue," available at http://www.americanprogress.org/issues/immigration/news/2013/05/28/64474/why-immigration-is-an-asian- american-issue/.

2. Pew Research Center, "The Rise of Asian Americans," available at http://www.pewsocialtrends.org/2012/06/19/the-rise-of-asian-americans/.
3. U.S. Department of Homeland Security, "Yearbook of Immigration Statistics: 2012" (Data Tables 40 and 41), available at http://www.dhs.gov/yearbook-immigration-statistics-2012-enforcement-actions.
4. Transactional Records Access Clearinghouse, Syracuse University.
5. South Asian Americans Leading Together (SAALT), *In Our Own Words: Narratives of South Asian New Yorkers Affected by Racial and Religious Profiling* (March 2012) available at http://saalt.org/wp- content/uploads/2012/09/In-Our-Own-Words-Narratives-of-South-Asian-New-Yorkers-Affected-by-Racial-and- Religious-Profiling.pdf.
6. Nermeen Arastu and Diala Shamas, *Mapping Muslims: NYPD Spying and Its Impact on American Muslims* (2013) available at http://www.law.cuny.edu/academics/clinics/immigration/clear/Mapping-Muslims.pdf.
7. South Asian Americans Leading Together (SAALT), *In Our Own Words: Narratives of South Asian New Yorkers Affected by Racial and Religious Profiling* (March 2012) available at http://saalt.org/wp-content/uploads/2012/09/In-Our-Own-Words-Narratives-of-South-Asian-New-Yorkers-Affected-by-Racial-and- Religious-Profiling.pdf.

CHAPTER 5: WHAT THE MEDIA SAY

"UNDOCUMENTED, NOT ILLEGAL: BEYOND THE RHETORIC OF IMMIGRATION COVERAGE," BY ANGELICA RUBIO

1. Monica Novoa, "Jose Antonio Vargas Came Out as Undocumented, NOT "Illegal," Colorlines, June 23, 2011.
2. Jose Antonio Vargas, "Jose Reports: View from Somewhere—A Real Conversation on Immigration," Define America, September 27, 2011.
3. David Holthouse and Mark Potok, "The Year In Hate, 2007," Southern Poverty Law Center, Spring 2008.

4. Jason DeParle, "The Anti-Immigrant Crusader," *New York Times*, April 17, 2011; Southern Poverty Law Center, "The Foundations: Funding the Greenwashers," July 2010; Federation for American Immigration Reform, "About," website.

5. Randal C. Archibold, "Arizona Enacts Stringent Law on Immigration," *New York Times*, April, 23, 2010; George Altman, "Alabama Immigration Law Poses Enforcement Challenges for Police," Alabama Live, November 5, 2011.

6. "Society of Professional Journalists Recommend Newsrooms Stop Using 'Illegal Alien,' Illegal Immigrant,'" *Huffington Post*, September 30, 2011.

7. Elena Shore, "How Do Ethnic Media Say, 'Illegal Immigrant?'" New America Media, News Report, September 19, 2011.

8. Seth Freed Wessler, "Bills Modeled After Arizona's SB 1070 Spread Through States," Colorlines, March 2, 2011.

9. Cristina Constantini, "Anti-Latino Hate Crimes Rise As Immigration Debate Intensifies," *Huffington Post*, October 18, 2011.

10. Ibid.

11. Ines Novacic, "Undocumented Irish Have No Trouble Finding Work in New York City," Irish Central, October 5, 2011.

12. Janet Murguia, "Join NCLR and the Drop Dobbs Campaign," *Huffington Post*, September 17, 2009.

13. Jeffrey S. Passel et al., "Hispanics Account for More Than Half of Nation's Growth in Past Decade," Pew Hispanic Center, March 24, 2011.

14. Vargas, "Jose Reports."

CONCLUSION

1. "On the Move: 232 Million Migrants Worldwide." *Guardian*. http://www.theguardian.com/news/datablog/2013/sep/11/on-the-move-232-million-migrants-in-the-world.

2. D'vera Cohen, "Future Immigration Will Change the Face of America by 2065." Pew Research Center, October 5, 2015. http://www.pewresearch.org/fact-tank/2015/10/05/future-immigration-will-change-the-face-of-america-by-2065.

GLOSSARY

alien—A term used to describe a person living in the United States illegally as a non-citizen. Some find this term culturally insensitive and prefer the more neutral term "undocumented."

asylee—One seeking asylum because of a well-founded fear of persecution based on one's political or religious beliefs, or on one's ethnicity in the former home nation.

CBP—An abbreviation for US Customs and Borders Protection.

DACA—Deferred Action for Childhood Arrivals, an immigration policy program launched in 2012.

DAPA—Deferred Action for Parents of Americans and Lawful Permanent Residents, an immigration policy program launched in 2014.

deferred action—The use of discretion to not deport an individual from the United States.

DHS—An abbreviation for the US Department of Homeland Security.

DOJ — An abbreviation for the US Department of Justice.

DOL—An abbreviation for the US Department of Labor.

E-Verify—An online system comparing information from Department of Homeland Security and Social Security Administration records to confirm employment authorization.

ICE—An abbreviation for US Immigration and Customs Enforcement.

lawful permanent resident—Any person not a citizen of the United States who is residing the in the United States under legally recognized permanent residence as an immigrant. Also known as a permanent resident alien, aresident alien permit holder, or a green card holder.

national of the United States—A person who, though not a citizen of the United States, owes permanent allegiance to the United States (e.g., persons born in American Samoa).

nonimmigrant—An alien who is admitted to the United States for a specific and temporary period of time.

permanent resident card (Form I-551)—Also known as the green card or alien registration card, this card is issued by USCIS to aliens as evidence of their lawful permanent resident status in the United States.

port of entry—Any location in the United States or its territories that is designated as a point of entry for aliens and US citizens.

refugee—A person outside his or her country of nationality who is unable or unwilling to return to that country because of persecution or a well-founded fear of persecution.

temporary protected status (TPS)—The Secretary of Homeland Security may designate a foreign country for TPS due to temporary conditions that prevent the country's nationals from returning safely.

US Citizenship and Immigration Services (USCIS)—A federal agency that oversees lawful immigration to the United States.

visa—A US visa allows the bearer to apply for entry to the United States under a certain classification (e.g. student (F), visitor (B), or temporary worker (H)).

FOR MORE INFORMATION

BOOKS

Eaton, Susan. *Integration Nation: Immigrants, Refugees, and America at Its Best*. New York: The New Press, 2015.

Gatrell, Peter. *The Making of the Modern Refugee*. Oxford, England: Oxford University Press, 2015.

Giordano, Cristiana. *Migrants in Translation: Caring and the Logics of Difference in Contemporary Italy*. Berkley, CA: University of California Press, 2014

Kershaw, Ian. *To Hell and Back: Europe, 1914-1949*. New York: Viking Press, 2015.

Nwadiuto, Buchi. *Refugee Crisis in Europe: Desperate Journeys*. Electronic Publication: Create Space Publications, 2015.

Patton, Kerry. *The Syria Report: The West's Destruction of Syria to Gain Control Over Iran*. New York: St. Martin's Press, 2013.

Sahner, Christian. *Among the Ruins: Syria Past and Present*. Oxford, England: Oxford University Press, 2014.

Tobin, Sarah. *The Syrian Refugee Crisis and Lessons from the Iraqi Refugee Experience*. Boston: Boston University Institute for Iraqi Studies, 2013.

Triandafyllidou, Anna. *Routledge Handbook of Immigration and Refugee Studies*. New York: Routledge, 2015.

Yazbek, Samar. *The Crossing: My Journey into the Shattered Heart of Syria*. London: Rider Books, 2015

WEBSITES

Center for Immigration Studies

www.cis.org

> CIS, or Center for Immigration Studies, is a nonprofit research center and influential conservative voice in the debate over US immigration policy. The group favors reduced legal and illegal immigration to the United States. Topics covered by the site include legislation, costs, national security, and wages, jobs, and poverty.

The National Council of La Raza

www.nclr.org

> Founded in 1968, The National Council of La Raza is the leading advocacy organization for Latino immigrants, who are by far the most numerous ethnicity processed through US immigration system. While self-identified as non-partisan, the group has a liberal orientation. Issues covered on their site include voting, education, civil rights, and health. La Raza also publishes longer publications, which can be linked from their site.

The Office of the United Nations High Commissioner for Refugees

www.unhcr.org

> Since 1950, the Office of the United Nations High Commissioner for Refugees has been the single most important conduit for information and policy regarding global refugee resettlement. Their website is the most comprehensive and informative source for all issues pertaining to refugees worldwide. Up-to-date facts and statistics, important definitions, articles, and more can be found on this site, and it is an essential resource for the ongoing refugee crisis.

INDEX

ABOUT THE EDITOR

Anne Cunningham has a PhD in comparative literature and has published articles on women modernist writers and feminist theory. She currently works as an instructor of English at the University of New Mexico – Taos. She is also a songwriter and performer, and lives with her husband and music partner, David Lerner, in Arroyo Hondo, NM.